UNLIMITED SLAUGHTER OF AMERICANS

UNLIMITED SLAUGHTER OF AMERICANS

By

Kerry Deminski

1stBooks - rev. 10/18/00

CHAPTER ONE

The *Parkerton Examiner* had a grand total of six employees and as Debra Dunn sat at her computer working on her story, the activities of the other five didn't even register in her mind. As always, when she was writing, her concentration was total. And it never mattered to her if the subject was subtle, shocking, or anywhere in between; she invariably instilled it with her own personal touch. Her current article dealt with a guide dog that had saved its owner's life when the sightless man was attacked near his home by a loose Rottweiler.

Debra glanced at her notebook and then finished the part of the story where the man had described to her how his dog had died in his arms as he knelt on the sidewalk. When she had interviewed him at his home earlier that afternoon, she had cried right along with him. So much for professionalism. Now tears started once again to slide down her cheeks. She sniffed as she reached for a tissue from the box she kept on her desk.

"Tough piece, Deb?" Jim Hopkins asked as he placed a comforting hand on her shoulder. Hopkins owned and edited the small-town daily. The teary-eyed reporter hadn't heard him approach, but wasn't embarrassed in the least as she turned to look up at him.

"Broke my heart, Jim," she admitted. She dabbed at her eyes and then wiped her nose before tossing the tissue into her wastebasket. "As soon as I finish the sympathy section here, I'll segue into my tirade about irresponsible dog owners and hope that some good might come out of this. That's why I love this job so much. But that's not news to you, right, Jim?" The publisher's face took on a rather painful expression. "Is something wrong?" she asked.

One of the female employees was walking by as Debra made this inquiry. She stopped and looked at her boss. It was no secret that the sixty-seven-year-old Hopkins had a history of

1

heart problems. "Are you okay, Jim? Are you having any pains?" the woman asked with a concerned look.

After a brief smile that both women thought was forced, he said, "Doc says I'm doing just fine. Just went to see him last week." The woman went on her way without looking convinced. "Debra, I'd like to talk with you in my office."

"Right now? Or should I finish this up first?" She looked briefly at the monitor screen. Jim Hopkins could see how anxious she was to transfer her words from her mind to the computer, but he hadn't the stomach for putting this off a moment longer. "Right now, Deb," he told her. She left the uncompleted article on the screen, saved it, and then followed her boss into his office.

"Close the door," he said, and then indicated that she should sit in the chair near his desk. Debra wasn't certain if it was her imagination, but he seemed to look ashen as he sat in his swivel chair behind the desk. He leaned forward and clasped his hands together as he placed them on the surface of his desk. After studying his hands for a few seconds, he looked up at Debra. He took a deep breath and then sighed. "Oh boy, I really hate to do this. I almost wish I could put all the blame on Tilly, but even though I'm doing this at her insistence, I have to admit that in my heart I know she's right. In the end it will be best for the both of us. You will be able to find a better job; you're too damn good a reporter not to. Debra, I'm sorry that I—"

"Tilly is making you fire me! But, Jim, I apologized to her about writing the story about her cousin passing all of those bad checks. Your wife told me not to worry about it. You were there. Remember how she said that even if you two hadn't been on vacation and had known what I was going to write, she wouldn't have asked you to kill the story. Tilly said her cousin deserved the notoriety as well as whatever legal punishment she'll get. I can't believe this. I really thought she appreciated what I've tried to do for your paper over the years. What hurts even more is that I always felt that she liked me as a person."

"Ah, Deb, you've got it all wrong. I'm not firing you. Tilly and I both love you like the daughter we were never able to have. Debra, I've sold the *Examiner*; I signed the final papers today."

This revelation stunned her even more than her suspected dismissal. "But why? Jim, you love this newspaper."

"I know. I always have. But ever since my heart problems started, Tilly has been worried about the stress—you know how I am about everything. And like I said, she's probably right. She's been so good to me for so many years. I honestly think I owe her this."

"What will you do? Are you going to live year-round in the home you own in Florida?"

He smiled. This one, she saw, was genuine. "Guilty. You know how much I enjoy the fishing down there. And Tilly has so many friends there as well."

"I can't believe this is happening," Debra said. "I'm going to miss you terribly. You've taught me so much about this business. And I'll never forget how kind you were to me when my marriage broke up. Then when my mother died exactly one week after my divorce was final, I must have been in here ten times a day crying on your shoulder." She leaned forward, clasped her hands together and then rested her chin on them. "I'd better change the subject before I start crying again. Do you think there's a chance that the new owner will keep any of us on?"

"This is the part that makes me feel like a real rat. The corporation is buying the paper to close it down in order to increase their circulation. They own the *Dispatch*." He colored slightly as he made the admission. "I feel somewhat like a traitor, selling out to our competitor, but, like I said, I'm not getting any healthier or younger, so I'll have to live with my guilt."

Debra leaned back in her chair. "You shouldn't feel guilty, Jim. You've worked harder than any of us to make the paper a success. You and Tilly both deserve to enjoy what you've earned."

"Thanks for understanding. Of all the gang here, I knew you'd be the one I could count on the most. That's why I asked you in first before I go out on the floor to drop the bomb on the rest of the crew." He looked at the door, knowing he should go out there and get it over with, but the urge to procrastinate was too strong. Also, the publisher's paternal feelings for the woman seated across from him prompted him to ask, "Do you think you'll finally make the decision to try your luck at getting hired by one of the major newspapers now that I've scuttled the *Examiner*?" Jim Hopkins had told Debra on many occasions that she was indeed talented enough to work for a paper in any major city in the country.

Debra sighed. "I'm afraid I'm too old and too comfortable here in my hometown to consider taking on a challenge like that."

"Come on, Deb. At thirty-six you've got a long way to go before you can even start thinking about being old. I'm betting you just don't want to bail out on your father."

She gave him a sad smile. "You know me too well, Jim. If Mom hadn't died, I wouldn't think twice about hounding editors all over the country for a job. But Dad seems so lost without her; I couldn't desert him as well. How could I live with myself if I did that to him?"

"Um, I don't know. The Bill Overfield I know would surely want his daughter to capitalize on her talent and be happy for her. Your dad is certainly not a selfish man."

"You're absolutely right. He would be totally supportive if I told him I had found a job in New York or Los Angeles or wherever. I can imagine how cheerful his letters and phone calls would be if I moved away. But, Jim, I can also imagine how depressed and lonely he would be living in that big old house all by himself."

"But your dad is such a young man. What is he, Deb, fifty-five, fifty-six?"

"He's only fifty-four. He had planned to retire from the post office on his fifty-fifth birthday and start traveling around the

4

country with my mom. It was hard to tell which one of them was more excited over the prospect." She lowered her head and began wringing her hands. He hoped she wasn't going to cry; he felt bad enough already over selling the paper.

"I don't want to sound cold-hearted, Deb, but do you think Bill might soon be ready to start dating again? Maybe then you could start your job search with a clear conscience."

Debra laughed. "I can't even find a nice guy I'd feel comfortable seeing, and you think my father can come up with a stepmother for me just like that?"

Jim chuckled. "I never mentioned marriage, young lady. Sounds like somebody is more of a daddy's girl than she cares to admit. Perhaps that's the real reason you're not too anxious to start knocking on the doors of all those big-city editors." He was smirking over his observation, but Debra was not at all offended.

"Tell you what, Jim. You find my dad a nice, respectable lady to keep him company before you move to Florida and I'll start sending out my resumes."

"Well, my dear, if I'm going to play Cupid, I just might set your daddy up with a beautiful young sex-pot instead of a nice, respectable lady."

"In that case, turn in your diaper and bow and arrow; you're fired," she said.

"Yep, I was right. You're a daddy's girl. You don't want him to have any fun. Now what have you got to say?"

"You big phony. Don't think I don't know what you're doing." Jim did his best to look innocent.

"You're just stalling for time because you hate to go out there and break the bad news to them," Debra said.

"I admit it. But there is one more thing I want to discuss with you first. Actually, two more things," he said. She made no comment as she waited to hear what else he wanted to tell her. Although slightly curious, she was certain neither disclosure could possibly come close to the magnitude of the news about the sale of the *Examiner*. "The first one concerns the Internet."

5

Debra smiled. "I know, you've gotten wind of a new Internet company that can make me an overnight millionaire if I invest in it." Hopkins was known to invest heavily—but not always wisely—in the stock market.

"No, wise guy, I was going to suggest that you give some strong consideration to starting your own newsletter on the Net. The way you dig into the human factor behind the news stories you cover deserves a much wider readership than you ever had here in Parkerton."

Debra gave a self-deprecating laugh. "Come on, Jim. I know I put my heart and soul into everything I write, but I don't believe that people would be willing to plunk down their cold hard cash for my work unless they also get sports, comics, and classifieds as part of the bargain."

"Well, that's part of my second suggestion, but don't make me get ahead of myself here, Deb."

"Boy, you sure sound like you've been putting an awful lot of time into worrying about my future. Too bad Pat didn't think I deserved that same amount of attention."

"Patrick Dunn was a total jerk," Jim said vehemently. "Correction: Your ex-husband *is* a total jerk and always will be. At least he got what he deserved. I sat right here and laughed my ass off when I heard that that bimbo he left you for dumped him three months after your divorce. No surprise he moved out of town with his tail between his legs after that happened. What does surprise me is that he didn't try to get you to take him back."

"Actually, Jim, he had tried. He called several times and sent me letters."

"He did? You never mentioned that before. Why didn't you tell me?" He was starting to breathe heavily and his color heightened as he thought of the prospect of his favorite employee screwing up her life with a man he couldn't stand.

"That's precisely why I didn't tell you. Now calm down, Jim. I hung up on him when he called and returned his letters without opening them. I may have been in love with Patrick

6

once, but I'd learned my lesson by then." She got up and filled a paper cup from the water cooler and handed it to him. "Do you need to take something with this? I don't want to sabotage your retirement with my disclosures about my ex. Tilly would get hold of me and slap me silly."

He did drink all of the water but took no medication. "Thanks. I feel better now. Getting back to what I was saying, I don't want you to sell yourself short and not look into my newsletter idea. I'm certain it wouldn't result in making you the overnight millionaire you mentioned in your snide reference to my investing skills, but I'm convinced there are many potential readers around the world who would become addicted to your style of writing."

"Debra Dunn, world-class journalist," she said mockingly. "Yeah, it has a nice ring to it. Won't you be sorry you sold the paper out from under me when I start getting accolades from countries we can't even find on the map."

"Talk about a hard sell. Okay, my second suggestion may be more to your liking. What would you say if I told you that your style of writing cries out for a syndicated column?"

"I would say that your guilt feelings over selling the paper is crying out to you and instructing you to give my writing ability credit it definitely doesn't deserve. Jim, I'll never forget how you took me under your wing and helped me to become the best reporter I can be. But my best just isn't as good as you think it is. Please don't misunderstand. I've loved every minute of working for you here at the *Examiner*. And I love you, Jim. I won't sit here and pretend that I don't know that I'm your favorite employee. But being teacher's pet hasn't clouded my judgement the way it's clouded yours. As flattering as your opinion of me is, Jim, editors and readers who don't live in our little town wouldn't possibly feel the same way about my talent for putting words on paper as you do."

"Oh no? Then why did Geoffrey Billings send me this contract with your name on it?" Jim Hopkins was pure Cheshire cat as he removed a thick stack of stapled papers from his middle drawer and then handed them across the desk to her.

She glanced at the first page, quickly scanned a few of the following pages, and then spent the most time studying the last page that contained Billings's signature as well as a blank line for hers. "But . . . but Geoffrey Billings runs the most successful syndicating company in the country. Parkerton, Indiana, may be only seventy-miles from Chicago, but I'm sure Billings would have no reason to visit here and read any of my articles in the *Examiner*. Why in the world would he be offering *me* a fantastic opportunity like this?" Debra asked. Jim Hopkins was immensely enjoying her dumbfounded expression.

"Hmm, let me think about that for a minute." Getting theatrical, Hopkins pursed his lips while he scratched his chin. "One of the reasons could be that I've been sending him copies of your stories ever since I became convinced that your insight and technique are special. Another reason could be that Geoff is no fool and didn't have to have his arm twisted to realize that a writer like you would be good for business. Oh, and last but not least, Geoff and I were college roommates and still go deep sea fishing together whenever we get the opportunity." He was positively beaming as he waited for her response.

"But why have you never mentioned your friendship with him to any of us at the paper?"

"We have a pact: I don't brag about the fact that I know him, and he doesn't brag about the fact that he knows me." He laughed. "No, seriously, I've known for some time now that I was going to sell the paper and I wanted this offer to dovetail with me doing the dastardly deed in order to salve my conscience. I've been fending Geoff off for the last six or seven months now because he's so anxious to get you on board."

"I feel like I'm dreaming all of this." She looked at the contract again. "He really thinks I deserve to be syndicated?"

"Oh, Debra. You see, that's the attitude that comes across so clearly in your writing. You can relate so well to the average person because you are convinced that you are an average person. And, for the love of God, don't ever change. No matter how successful you may become, don't turn into one of those glitzy, know-it-all types who treat fame as his or her due. Stay humble, stay focused, stay caring—in short—stay you."

"Jim, I hope you realize how grateful I am. And not only for this." She held up the contract for a few seconds before placing it back on her lap. "I truly appreciate everything you've ever done for me. I . . . I think I'm going to cry." Her self-fulfilling prophecy was immediately followed by tears welling up and escaping her eyes.

He wasted no time in getting to his feet. After coughing once to try to do something about the lump in his throat, he said, "That's my cue to exit. I'm going out on the floor and deliver the bad news."

She waylaid him to deliver a tight hug as soon as he rounded his desk. "Jim, would you please not tell them about my contract?" Those papers were clutched in one of her hands behind his back. "I don't want them to hear my good news and their bad news at the same time."

"I wasn't going to. You can decide when the time is right." He disengaged himself from her embrace and took a step back. "Just sit back down and get yourself together." She took his advice—at least the part about sitting. Jim put a hand on her shoulder and said, "Don't take too long, though; we have a deadline and you have a story to finish writing."

She looked up at him and smiled. He squeezed her shoulder and then left his office.

Kerry Deminski

CHAPTER TWO

Breakfast at the Cordell household was choreographed as smoothly by Elaine Cordell as all of her routines had been when she was a professional skater. Despite the fact that she now maneuvered on linoleum between stove, refrigerator and table instead of gliding on ice in a sequined costume, she handled her task with noticeable grace. Her husband, Ryan, watched her movements with undisguised admiration. "And what do you find so interesting this morning?" she asked as she made her way around the table while pouring orange juice into four glasses.

Ryan wrapped an arm around her waist as she filled his glass. "The prettiest woman in the state of Illinois," he replied with no hesitation.

She spun out of his embrace as well as out of his reach. "And I bet I'm supposed to think that your flattery has absolutely nothing to do with the fact that you'll be spending the major part of your day with Rebecca Sinclair. Hah! You've been ogling that little strumpet ever since she started doing the news on TV."

"Mommy, is a strumpet a lady that plays a trumpet?" Caitlin asked as she walked into the kitchen.

Ryan laughed as his wife turned to look at their six-year-old daughter. "Come on, Mommy, answer our innocent little angel's question," he said.

Elaine shot her husband a nasty look before turning back to her daughter. "No, sweetheart. A strumpet is a woman who sells things."

"What kind of things?"

"She sells favors."

"Oh, like party favors. That must be a fun job," Caitlin said as she sat on her usual chair.

"You can say that again," Ryan said with a smirk.

"Say what again?" Luke asked as he walked in and took a seat across the table from his sister.

"Mommy, was just telling me about what strumpets sell," Caitlin explained.

Luke gave his mother a look of shock and disapproval. He was fourteen, a loner who was a voracious reader and had come across that old-fashioned term for a prostitute on numerous occasions. Before Elaine offered a clarification of her action, Caitlin said, "Strumpets are ladies who sell party favors, Luke." The girl took a sip of her orange juice before pouring syrup on her waffle.

Luke may have been a newcomer to the conversation, but he simply had to take the opportunity to let his parents know how insightful he was. "So, Dad, isn't today the day that hot-looking TV reporter is going to interview you at the factory?" He gave his mother his most innocent look before turning back to hear his father's reply.

"I do believe you're right, Luke," Ryan said.

"Would you mind asking her what kind of favors she'd recommend for my next birthday party?" Luke asked his father.

"Oh, the two of you are simply hilarious," Elaine said as both her husband and her son smiled at their perceived cleverness. "I bet you won't think it's so funny if she badmouths both your factory and your organization." She sat and began to eat her breakfast.

"I might have similar concerns about the interview had I agreed to do it live," he told her. "Even though Rebecca Sinclair augments her income by selling party favors on the side," Ryan said as he gave his daughter a brief smile, which she returned, "you can never be certain that a TV reporter won't ambush you during an interview. Since we own a sizable chunk of the local TV channel that Sinclair works for, I had no problem in getting the green light to okay the footage before it's aired." He wiped a drop of maple syrup from the corner of his mouth before giving his wife what he thought was a grin, but she interpreted it as a smirk.

"Just don't forget that that is *all* you have the green light to do," Elaine advised her husband as she viciously stabbed a piece of her waffle before placing it in her mouth.

"It's times like this when I can't help but wonder if you're ever going to get beyond all of the competitiveness that won you so many championships before you turned pro," Ryan observed.

"I'm going to win a lot of championships before I turn pro, Daddy," Caitlin said with more than a little determination.

"I bet you will, sweetheart," Ryan said with not a trace of condescension in either his voice or his mind. "You're going to be a great skater and you have a great skater teaching you."

Elaine spent as much time as possible on the ice with her daughter as she passed along all of the skills the youngster was capable of assimilating. Although Luke had never expressed any desire to even put on a pair of ice skates, Caitlin had asked for her first pair at the age of three after seeing one of her mother's videotapes for the first time. Since then, Caitlin had seen all of the tapes in Elaine's sizable collection. She knew all of the words that described the moves her mother executed and begged Elaine to teach all of them to her. Naturally, due to Caitlin's age and limited strength, Elaine had to be selective in what she allowed her daughter to attempt.

"I'm simply going to ignore that latest attempt at flattering me into complacency," Elaine told her husband. "My warning still stands. Behave yourself today or else."

"You know I don't take kindly to ultimatums," Ryan said. "Just for that I'm going to flirt my butt off today with Rebecca Sinclair."

"You're silly," Caitlin advised her father.

Ryan made no rebuttal to his daughter's statement. Elaine merely uttered a barely audible, "Humph." Luke, on the other hand, gave his father a brief sideways glance that went unnoticed by all of the others seated around the table. Had the other family members seen it—at least his parents—they would have noted that he regarded his father with envy. Luke fervently wished that he could project even a modicum of the confidence that his

13

father displayed. True, Luke clearly was going to be tall like his dad—he was already only a quarter of an inch short of five eleven, but it was height without the corresponding weight. He was small-boned like his mother, and almost painfully thin in the bargain. Since he had so far been unable to tolerate wearing contact lenses, his poor vision necessitated the wearing of glasses with rather thick lenses. His journey toward manhood was not made any easier by the taunting of the teenage boys in high school. He fared no better with the girls he encountered. Even though his IQ was above average, he didn't have to be in the genius category to realize that none of the girls found him to be even remotely attractive.

Luke Cordell was not one to wallow in self-pity. Perhaps he was destined to be virtually friendless as he made it through his high school years, but he had something he suspected that few, if any, of his classmates had. Whenever he was reading the fiction that consumed so much of his spare time, he was never lonely, he was never homely, he was never lacking in confidence. He not only identified with the brave and handsome men who populated those novels and short stories, he *was* those men. He glorified in every wrong he righted, in every villain he dispatched, in every woman he loved. It was only when the books were closed and he functioned as best he could in the debilitating world of teenage angst that he felt so uncompromisingly miserable.

One oasis amid that misery was his English class in which American literature was currently being studied. Jared Bernstein taught the class, and Luke admired the man with a passion. Not only did the perceptive teacher immediately discern that Luke had an appreciation for literature that was rare in a person his age, Bernstein intuitively knew that it was better for the boy to display his love and understanding of fiction in his written work instead of having him demonstrate it orally. Bernstein had invited Luke to participate in the after-school sessions he held on Fridays for those students who had a more than average liking for the written word. It was during those sessions, which included students from all four grades in high school, that he called upon Luke to speak out. And Luke did so with no trepidation. Even though he hadn't formed any friendships with these like-minded students, Luke felt as though he could share his love of reading with no fear of ridicule. It was after one of these sessions ended that he had waited until all of the other kids had left before blurting out to Jared Bernstein that he planned to devote his life to writing fiction after he graduated from college. This plan for his future was so close to his heart that Luke had shared it with no one else in the world. To his credit, Bernstein, who was a frustrated and as-yet unpublished writer, offered only encouragement. Luke had been beaming as he'd left the classroom on that fateful Friday afternoon. All the way home he entertained fantasies of presenting his beloved mentor with a signed copy of his first published novel.

Luke got up from the breakfast table and started to walk away, but stopped when his mother said, "You haven't even eaten half of your food. Luke, I'm going to take you back to the pediatrician if you don't start eating more."

"Mom, I'm just not all that hungry. And I'm too old to be going to a pediatrician."

"No, you're not. I'm not going to have you getting any thinner than you already are. Look at your sister; Caitlin eats twice as much as you do."

"Yeah, and she's also skinnier than I am. Why don't you take her to the pediatrician?"

"Because she's a girl and she's only six. You're fourteen, Luke." Elaine turned to her husband for support. "Ryan, can't you convince our son eat more and perhaps do some exercise to bulk up? I know you're not interested in any sports, Luke, but maybe you could do some weight training."

"Isn't it enough that you have Caitlin brainwashed into wanting to be a champion ice skater like you were? Why can't you just keep spending all of your time with her like you always do and leave me alone?" Once again he headed out of the room.

Ryan saw the hurt look on his wife's face as well as the way his son's shoulders slumped dejectedly as he exited. The look he gave his wife was anything but accusatory, yet she felt compelled to say, "Do you think I was wrong? We've been taking him to Doctor Metcalf since he was born." She looked at the doorway through which Luke had departed. "And it's not my fault that Caitlin wants to skate and he only enjoys reading and hates sports."

"Of course it's not your fault," Ryan agreed as he pushed back his chair and stood. "I'm going to talk with him."

Before Ryan got out of hearing range he heard Caitlin tell her mother, "I would rather skate by myself like you did, but I would skate partners with Luke if he ever wanted me to." As he began climbing the stairs, Ryan thought that the unsolicited unselfish statement by his daughter should take away at least part of the sting of the brainwashing accusation.

Luke was in the process of closing the door to his bedroom when Ryan said, "Luke, I'd like to talk to you for a minute. Do you mind if I come in?"

Luke opened the door all the way and stepped aside. "No, but would you rather do this in your office?"

Ryan stopped just inside the doorway. "Do what in my office?"

"Yell at me for mouthing off at Mom. Isn't that why she sent you up here?"

"Your mother didn't *send* me anywhere, Luke. She is down there wondering if perhaps you are too old to continue going to Doctor Metcalf. I wouldn't be surprised if she's also a little upset over what you said about her and your sister."

"I know. I'm sorry I said that," Luke admitted.

"Your mom is the one you should be saying that to instead of me."

"Yeah, I'll tell her before I leave for school. I probably sounded jealous of all the time she spends at the rink with Caitlin, but I'm really not. It's just that she sometimes makes me feel guilty because I'm not the athlete that she is."

"I honestly don't think that's her intention, Luke." Luke walked over to his bed and sat on the edge. Ryan rolled the swivel chair away from his son's computer desk, turned it toward the bed and sat.

"I wish I was built more like you instead of being skinny like Mom and Caitlin. Maybe then she wouldn't be picking on me about not eating enough."

"Um, I would have to say that your mother's comments this morning were made only because she's concerned about your health. And I gotta tell you, Luke, I think she's right."

"Oh, great," Luke said sarcastically. "Now you agree with her that I should be going back to my baby doctor. Do you have any idea how dorky I'm going to feel sitting in a waiting room full of rug rats?" Ryan laughed. "I bet you wouldn't think it was so funny if you were my age and your parents forced you to go to a pediatrician."

"In my opinion, Doctor Metcalf is a very qualified physician, but I tend to agree with you on this one. I think the next time you need to see a doctor I'll take you to Doctor Lewis. I believe you'd like him."

"You will? You'll take me to your doctor?"

"Why not? But don't get too excited. The part of your mother's statement I was talking about was having you get more exercise. I'm not convinced you need to get any medical attention at this point."

"Oh. So then you want me to join a YMCA or a health club or something?"

"Well, you could if you want to. But since our town doesn't have either one, I was thinking more along the lines of getting a few pieces of exercise equipment and possibly some weights for one of the rooms in the basement. That way I could work out with you without having your mom accusing me of flirting with any women at a health club like she's getting on my case about Rebecca Sinclair." Ryan looked around the room at the hundreds of books that lined the shelves he'd had built in to accommodate his son's passion for reading. "Do you think you could tear yourself away from your hobby a few hours a week in order to bulk up a little and make your mother happy?"

"Dad, I don't want to work in your company after I go to college." Luke looked apprehensive after making the announcement.

"Where did that come from?" Ryan asked.

"You called my reading a hobby, but it's more than that. Dad, I want to go to college and then become a writer. I want to write novels. I'm sorry."

"Sorry? Why in the world is that something to be sorry about?"

"Well, you inherited the factory from your father and then built it up into the most successful business in our town. I just assumed you would be mad at me when you found out I didn't want to work there and learn the business like you did. I wasn't going to tell you how I felt until I was ready to graduate from college, because I didn't want you to be disappointed in me any longer than you had to be. I don't know why I blurted it out now. I wish I had kept my big mouth shut about it."

"Oh boy," Ryan said. "How long have you been keeping this secret from us?"

"I'm not sure. At least a couple of years. I didn't want to hurt your feelings."

"You wouldn't have hurt my feelings had you told me this while you were in college, and you haven't hurt my feelings now."

"I haven't?"

"Of course not. Just because I happen to enjoy running the company doesn't give me the right to expect either your sister or you to enjoy running it when the time comes for it to belong to both of you. There are plenty of management types out there who would be delighted to do the work while you and Caitlin do whatever makes you happy." Ryan chuckled. "But I have to warn you, Luke, I intend to run the business until the day I drop dead, so don't get any ideas about packing me off to a retirement home and hiring that manager while I'm still breathing."

"Don't sweat it, Dad. I'll be perfectly content to be a starving writer living in some decrepit rooming house as long as you're not mad at me for not joining your company. Now I'm really glad I did tell you what I want to do with my life. I haven't felt so happy in a long time."

"I'm glad to hear that. But if you want to keep your mother happy, you'd better not mention any plans to starve in the future."

Luke grinned. "Yeah, I can picture her sitting with me in the pediatrician's waiting room when I'm thirty."

Ryan smiled at his son and then checked his watch. He stood and said, "I really have to be on my way and make sure everything is ready for that interview today. But before I go, there's something else I want to tell you. When I was your age, I was fortunate enough to know exactly what I wanted to do with my life. Although the factory was much smaller then, I was already spending as much time in it as you spend reading. I never had any doubts in my mind about my future because my father had already told me that he was teaching me all about his business because it would be mine in the future. I'm sure you know that I'm extremely proud of what I do for a living, and I want you to know that I'm equally proud of what you want to do for a career. Creating plots and characters that will not only entertain people but will also make them laugh and cry—both essential emotions, is an important way to spend your time. As romantic a notion as it is to be struggling in that decrepit rooming house you mentioned, I'd prefer to give you an option. I'm going to set up a trust fund that will kick in the day you graduate from college. That way you can devote your time to writing and work only if you choose to do so for background material for your novels. Now I'm not too sure if Caitlin will follow through with her plans to become a professional skater, but since you seem to have a knack for feeling guilty, I'll set up a trust fund for her as well." He looked at his watch again. "Luke, I really have to leave. Thanks for telling me about your plans. You made my day. Luke Cordell, world-famous author. I don't know about you, but I like the sound of that."

Ryan smiled at his son, who appeared to be almost in a state of shock as he sat on his bed in silence, and then turned and walked quickly out of the bedroom.

When Ryan Cordell was notified by his secretary that Rebecca Sinclair was already outside his office, he wondered why she was there a half-hour early. As soon as she walked inside and closed the door she brought his speculation to an end. "Mr. Cordell, I just found out from my producer that he wants me to turn this interview into a lovefest and I want you to know that I'm totally pissed off about it." Being totally pissed off took absolutely nothing away from how beautiful she looks, Ryan thought. And even though he had never once given Elaine a reason not to trust him during their entire marriage, it was easy to understand her warning at the breakfast table.

"And a good morning to you too, Ms. Sinclair," he said, and followed that with a disarming smile. "Shall we shake hands and come out fighting?" He extended his hand while keeping his smile in place.

Rebecca briefly shook his hand, but no way was she going to return the smile. "I spent most of last night working on hard-hitting questions about workplace violence, gun control, and the murder rate in this country compared to the rest of the world. And now, thanks to orders from my boss, I can't use a single one of them. I was so furious I came this close to quitting," she said as she held a thumb and index finger a tiny bit apart in front of her face. "I'm a news reporter, damn it, and this isn't news."

"I'm sure it would be if you had your crew in here to record this," he said, refusing to be ruffled by her outburst. "Do you have them cooling their heels in my secretary's office while you read me the riot act?"

"We're going to fix you up with a lavaliere mike. My 'crew' consists only of my cameraman who is doing exterior shots.

After he's finished he will be out there chatting up your secretary until we're ready to start taping."

He got up and walked over to an alcove. "I'm going to have a cup of coffee; would you like some?" he asked. "I'm sure that being this mad this early in the day calls for some added caffeine intake. Cream? Sugar?" He stood by the counter in the alcove as he waited for her reply.

"What are you trying to do? Charm me into being happy about getting into bed with a firearms manufacturer?"

"I'm so glad my wife didn't hear that. Even though I'm old enough to be your father and you were speaking figuratively, I don't think she could handle it." He turned back toward the counter and busied himself with the drinks. When he walked back into the office he handed her one of the mugs. "I gave you cream and two sugars; I think you could use a few extra pounds. I have some cinnamon rolls in there as well if you'd like one." She accepted the coffee and also sat in the chair he motioned to. He moved the remaining visitor's chair to face hers and sat there instead of retreating to the power seat behind the desk.

She took a sip of the coffee and then looked at him over the rim of her mug. "Um, this is good."

"Yes, isn't it? Are you certain you wouldn't like me to get you one of those rolls to go with it?"

"As tempting as that sounds, no thanks. I shouldn't even be having this," she said and then immediately took a few swallows. "What is this, some kind of special blend?"

"As a matter of fact, it is." He grinned. "But don't worry; I haven't added any witch's potion that will prevent you from continuing to be mad at me."

"I'm not mad at you. I'm mad at myself for not fighting harder with my producer about turning this interview into a puff piece."

"That would have been a losing battle. I'm sure you were told that I agreed to do this only if I had final approval to ascertain that neither the company nor the organization was vilified."

"That's true. But by adhering to the rules that were laid down to me this morning, I'm afraid this piece will come off sounding like an infomercial instead of a news segment. I realize that your company is our town's biggest employer and that Thomasville would be hurt financially if you ever decided to move your operation elsewhere. And yet I have to admit that I don't respect my boss as much today as I did yesterday. He should have allowed me to do a more insightful piece that reflects the opinions of most Americans."

"Including yours?"

"Including mine," she answered truthfully.

"Rebecca . . . you don't mind if I get less formal here and use your first name, do you? Charge it up to my advanced age and not the fact that the Cordell Firearms Company is Thomasville's biggest employer."

That elicited a smile from her. "I read your bio; forty-five is hardly a doddering senior citizen."

"Oh, I've been known to dodder after a long, hard day around here. Anyway, I'd really appreciate it if you wouldn't be too hard on your producer. When we discussed doing this, he agreed with me that my company has a lot of people in and around Thomasville who understand that the quality weapons we produce are put to good—and I might add, legal—use by customers all around the world."

"That's true," she agreed, "but even you would have to admit that many weapons that are purchased for self-protection or hunting are often used to murder lovers, wives and other family members."

"No, I disagree with your use of the word 'often' here—and statistics will back me up—but I will concede that legally-purchased weapons are sometimes used for illegal purposes." He took a sip of coffee and waited for her to continue.

"But what about the weapons sold on the street? And then you have the burglaries of gun shops and private homes during which weapons are stolen for use in violent crimes."

"Yes," he said, "and in a perfect world, none of these crimes would be committed." After setting his mug on the blotter on his desk, Ryan said, "I also read your bio, Rebecca, so I know that you were born and raised in Gosper, Nebraska, a town with about two thousand citizens. I'm positive that your friends and relatives back in Gosper don't feel the need to have weapons in their homes or carry them on their persons for self-protection. But I can guarantee that many law-abiding people living in Miami, or Chicago, or New York, or any other major city don't have that luxury of feeling safe at home or in public. The people who work for me are proud of what we do for those law-abiding people, and so am I."

Since she was much more interested in the conversation than she was in the delicious coffee, Rebecca also placed her mug on the desk. She leaned slightly forward as she asked, "All that may be so, but how can you justify the organization you've founded? I've read some of the letters your members send to your monthly publication, and, quite frankly, they scare me. It seems that most of those characters are spoiling to have shootouts with each and every branch of the government. Surely even you have to find that disturbing."

"Again, I'll have to disagree. For every member who wants to air his views in our publication, there are countless others who are content to merely sit back and realize that their contributions are being wisely used to do whatever is necessary to keep it legal for responsible citizens to own firearms. I know for a fact that many of our members are as offended by some of the letters sent in by others as you are. In fact, more than a few have threatened to drop out of the organization because of it, and a handful have carried out those threats."

"Then why in the world do you continue to publish the belligerent letters? Wouldn't it make good economic sense to weed them out or, at the very least, edit them to the point where they're less bombastic? And speaking of editing, some of the grammar in the more offensive letters is absolutely appalling. Why don't you have your staff members assure that the writing

23

appears not to have been written by such poorly-educated people?"

Ryan chuckled and then glanced at his watch. "Surely your guy has finished all of his exterior shots by now. Aren't you going to get him mad by keeping him waiting while you and I sit here chatting and enjoying this coffee, which is getting too cool for my taste." He picked up his mug, finished its contents, and put it back on his desk.

"He's getting paid by the hour." Rebecca said nothing else until she, too, finished her coffee. "You, on the other hand, no doubt want to get to the softball interview that I've been order to conduct. And, by the way, I also read that you're the major shareholder of the company I work for. That's another big reason why this virtual gag order has left such a bitter taste in my mouth."

"Maybe I should have given you three sugars instead of two in your coffee," he said with a completely straight face.

She couldn't help grinning at that. "You can sit here and make cutesy remarks now, but I wouldn't be surprised if you call up my boss as soon as I drive away and use your clout to get me fired. Since you are the big fish in the little pond here in Thomasville, I bet that's precisely the reason you invested so heavily in Channel Two. Now you never have to worry about any of our reports being unfavorable."

"Aren't you reporters supposed to be asking questions instead of making statements?" He wasn't smiling, but she could clearly see the humor in his eyes. "Anyway, you have nothing at all to worry about insofar as your job security is concerned. I know that you're a news reporter and that what I've agreed to do today hardly qualifies as news. But let's say, hypothetically, of course, that you were here to talk to me because I'd gotten drunk last night and drove my car through the window of Bloombergs' Delicatessen on Main Street. Even if you used the awesome power of local television news to humiliate me even further, I would do nothing to jeopardize your career for merely doing your job. The only reason I bought the stock in the TV outlet was because the town wasn't yet wired for cable TV and I wanted them to show more ice skating shows to make my wife happy."

"That is so romantic," she said. "I'd heard that you built the skating rink in town a few years ago because your daughter wanted to learn to skate, but I didn't know about the TV outlet."

"Well, now that you do, don't spread it around. If those grammar-deficient members of GUN that you mentioned find out that I'm a big softy, they'll switch back to the NRA. Which reminds me, I don't edit their letters because prettying them up would not serve any useful purpose. They would probably think I was criticizing their beliefs as well as their limited understanding of the English language. I believe it's far better for that segment of the population to have a forum to get those feelings expressed as opposed to grousing in private. My sincere hope is that not a single one of our members ever does anything remotely resembling anarchy, but should that occur, it's a foregone conclusion that the government is monitoring our publication and would waste no time in knocking on my door for information."

"And you would hand over that information without protest?"

"I would indeed. GUN is all about maintaining the freedom to bear arms, not the freedom to break the law."

"How did you come up with the acronym for your organization?"

"I was reading an article in one of the papers about workplace violence. The reporter theorized that the government should outlaw the ownership of firearms by all private citizens and thereby end the problem in the country. I was furious over how ridiculous that simplistic—not to mention—unworkable approach would be. Even if I hadn't inherited the company, I still would not want the longstanding tradition of hunting and target shooting in the country to end simply because a tiny fraction of the population can't control their emotions. To me, giving up that tradition was unthinkable. Give up? Never! And that was it; I had my acronym as well as my reason for starting the not-for-profit organization."

As they sat leaning against pillows positioned against the headboard of their king-size bed, Elaine and Ryan Cordell watched the end of the segment that had been taped at his company and organization headquarters. The image of Rebecca Sinclair in the studio once again appeared on the TV screen. "Although I still feel that our country needs even more stringent gun-control laws to further our safety, I came away from that encounter with Ryan Cordell with a deeper understanding of the man who owns the Cordell Firearms Company and who founded the GUN organization. I am positive that Mister Cordell sincerely believes, in his mind and in his heart, that the rights of responsible citizens to own firearms should not—must not—be taken from them. It was his sincerity, and not his palpable charisma, that gave me a clearer comprehension of the pride taken by Ryan Cordell and all of his employees in the work that they do.

"I'm Rebecca Sinclair. All of us here at Channel Two News thank you for watching and we'll see you again tomorrow night."

"Leno or Letterman?" Ryan asked as he aimed the remote at the television set.

"Conversation," Elaine stated as she reached over and depressed the "OFF" button without taking the remote out of his hand. "Where does that little bitch get the right to talk about your so-called 'palpable charisma'? What the hell was that all about? What went on between the two of you today? And why did you record that? Didn't you see enough of the slut today?"

"Sh, you're going to wake up Caitlin," he cautioned.

"I don't give a damn who I wake up! Give me that remote; I'm going to erase that tape."

He held the remote off the side of the bed and well out of her reach. "Come on, Elaine. You know that I always record myself whenever I'm on TV so that I can see what I did wrong and correct it the next time. And you shouldn't be complaining about my tape. You must have a few hundred tapes of your performances. And, I might add, your tapes show a lot of your cleavage as well as most of your butt, which can hardly be said of Rebecca Sinclair on this footage."

"That's entirely different, and you know it. Don't you sit there with that smug look on your face, Ryan. Don't try to get me to believe that you weren't looking at that beautiful young woman and wishing you could do it with her."

"Do you know just how young she is?" he asked.

"Too young."

"She's twenty-five. And when I was looking at her I was picturing our Caitlin at her age and wondering if she would have accomplished her skating goals. I'm afraid I'm never going to be one of those men who thinks he's attractive to young women no matter how old he gets. All I am is a guy who will never be able to get over being attracted to you no matter how old you get. But I have to tell you, seeing you act jealous like that makes me really, and I mean *really*, want to make love to you."

She looked at him for a moment before saying, "Put down the remote and turn out the light." As soon as he performed both tasks, she said, "Come here, Mister Palpable Charisma."

Kerry Deminski

CHAPTER THREE

The number of shoppers in the Value Plus supermarket was fairly small even for a day so near to the end of the month. And that suited the checkout clerk on register 3 just fine. Laura Porter wasn't in the mood to deal with an endless stream of customers on this particular morning. The left side of her face was still slightly swollen, but she had applied enough makeup to make the bruise barely discernible. Last night had been the first time her live-in boyfriend had ever hit her, and she vowed it would be the last. She ejected Ray Faleski from her apartment and from her life within minutes after he punched her. He was extremely reluctant to go, but with his record of arrests, he began gathering up his meager belongings as soon as she threatened to call 911. Their relationship had lasted for fourteen months and she had truly cared for him, but now admitted to herself that her attempts to turn his life around had been a dismal failure. Laura had too much self-respect to become any man's punching bag.

Another customer began placing her groceries on the conveyor belt and Laura started to slide the items over the window of the scanner. The beeping punctuated her thoughts of the good and bad times she had spent with Ray. He was six years older than her twenty-two and ruggedly handsome. She had admitted to herself on more than one occasion that she was shallow enough to let his good looks overshadow his mercurial temper. But being yelled at and belittled was one thing; being hit was entirely something else. She had lost count of the jobs he had been fired from or quit since they'd been together. What had precipitated yesterday's argument was his being fired from the Value Plus where she worked. She had practically begged her manager to give him the job, and Ray had been fired for stealing high-priced food items, which he sold.

"Miss, are you going to take my money?" the woman asked as she held the four twenty-dollar bills toward Laura.

"Sorry about that," Laura said as she began to concentrate once again on the present instead of the past. She rang up the sale and then gave the woman her change.

"You look kind of out of it, Laura," her manager said. He had been walking nearby when the slightly-annoyed woman summoned Laura out of her reverie. "I know you're upset because I had to let your boyfriend go. But I hope you realize that I had no choice in the matter." She was about to tell him that she completely understood and that she had broken it off with Ray. "Laura, what happened to your face?" He immediately looked angry. "Did he do that to you?"

"Yes, Ted, he punched me last night when I told him to move out." She ran her fingers lightly over her swollen cheek. "I'm not going to let him hurt me ever again."

"Hey, Ted, I have something for you," Ray Faleski said as he walked quickly toward the two of them.

"Ray! No!" Laura shouted as her former lover pulled a pistol out of his coat. The manager spun around to see and hear the weapon at the same time. He was already falling before his look of surprise changed to a grimace of pain. "Ray! Stop that!" she shouted again as he fired two more rounds into the man's body. "Ray! Are you crazy?"

"Good-bye, Laura," he said as he aimed his weapon at her chest and pulled the trigger. Her expression was a study in disbelief as he sent a second round into her chest.

Laura Porter sank out of sight. The only other register that was open was the one nearest the automatic doors. The middle-aged woman who had been calmly putting her items on that conveyor belt began screaming as soon as the gunfire erupted. A second before Ray Faleski pivoted toward the sound, the register clerk dove out of sight beneath her counter. Hiding was not an option for the frightened customer. She bolted for the door, but fell to the floor when a round shattered the bone in her right thigh. Faleski walked calmly to the fallen woman, leaned down and pressed the pistol against the back of her head. Her body jerked violently as he squeezed the trigger and then it lay still.

The screams of a hysterical woman erupted from one of the aisles in the store. Faleski knew he should run out to his car and escape, but the blood lust was too strong. He ignored the clerk trembling beneath the counter at register 1 and sprinted toward the screamer.

A man who had just pulled into a parking space facing the supermarket and had seen the three shootings snatched up his cell phone to call the police. Even as he spoke with the 911 operator, he was formulating a plan of action. With help on the way, he put his car into reverse and backed up into a space that had a clear view of the doors. Since he carried no weapons, his plan was to use his vehicle to run into the man and dispense vigilante justice if the gunman bolted before the police arrived. He'd be damned if he'd let the gunman escape after the horror he'd just witnessed.

The woman who had screamed attracted the attention of the only butcher on duty. He had just begun placing packages of ground chuck into a display case through a window from his cold domain. Although he'd opened the sliding window a second after the shots had been fired and hadn't heard them, he saw Faleski walking rapidly toward the woman who had screamed. His darting eyes also took in the pistol in Ray Faleski's hand, the fear on the young woman's face and the baby lying inside her shopping cart in a plastic carrier. When the gunman's head swiveled toward the butcher, the man instantly slammed the mirrored window shut.

"Don't shoot!" the woman shouted. "Please don't shoot me!" She was able to plead for her life, but fear had rendered her incapable of moving. Faleski's pace slowed as he neared the terrified woman. He was totally in control of the situation as he aimed the pistol at the center of her chest. Her eyes lowered to the weapon for less than a second before returning to his face. He could not help smiling as his finger began to apply pressure on the trigger. Had he known that the emotional high of taking human lives was so intense, he would have done so sooner.

"Help me!" the woman screamed as her head pivoted to watch the butcher explode through swinging doors with a meat cleaver raised above his shoulder. As fast as the would-be rescuer was, Faleski was faster. He fired three rounds in rapid succession into the man's chest. As he pitched forward onto the floor, the cleaver fell from his grasp, slid into one of the wheels of the woman's shopping cart, and then spun around several times before becoming motionless. Equally motionless was the man sprawled on the floor as his blood began seeping from beneath his white apron.

Ray Faleski reloaded the pistol and then turned back toward the woman. Although her baby was now crying after being startled by the gunfire, the woman was staring silently at the butcher's body. Faleski was angry now. Not at the woman, but at the man who would surely have split his head in two had not the woman stupidly warned him of the threat. He rewarded her by shooting her while her eyes were not on him and his weapon. While watching her slump gracefully to the floor, he knew he had wounded her fatally with a heart shot and wouldn't have to finish her off as he did with the other female customer.

The only other human in his field of vision was the baby, who was now wailing even louder. Ray knew that the mother's death was not comprehended by one so young. He took a few steps forward and bent his head to look at the baby. A pink headband above the tightly-closed eyes that shed copious tears told him the baby was a girl. For a brief moment he looked down at the mother and thought about how close his mother and his only sister had always been. He had never once begrudged them that closeness, but he had spent countless nights longing for a similar bond with a father who had deserted the family before he'd been born. There was no way he was going to allow the same emotional agony to befall the crying baby. One more step brought him close enough to position the barrel of the pistol right against the headband in the center of her forehead. The round tore right through the headband without severing it. It did penetrate the plastic baby seat as well as the cart—also plastic—and embedded itself in the floor.

After stepping around the carnage, Faleski decided to continue to the rear of the store and reconnoiter each aisle to eliminate any possible eyewitnesses. Each aisle was empty until he got to the next to last one. An elderly lady, looking to be in her eighties or nineties, was calmly taking cans of cat food off the shelves and placing them into her cart. She was so engrossed in her task that she didn't notice him as he stood for a few seconds at the end of the aisle and watched her. He walked to the final aisle, saw no one there and then returned to the pet food aisle.

Faleski was only a few feet away from the elderly shopper when she finally noticed him. She flinched and then smiled. "Oh, you startled me. I don't hear very well these days." The woman also didn't see as well as she once had; the gun in his hand went unnoticed. "Young man, would you be a dear and reach up there to get me two cans of the beef and chicken blend. My little Patches just loves that flavor." Because the woman was so short and he was standing so close, Faleski misjudged and shot her in the abdomen instead of the chest. Since she weighed less than ninety pounds, the round went right through her and knocked several cans of cat food off the shelves. "Ow! What did you do to me?" He answered her question by adjusting his aim a little higher. Because this lady might be a particularly tough one, he did follow up the two torso shots with one in the head. No point in taking any unnecessary chances.

It was at that point that Ray Faleski remembered the clerk who had crouched down at her register when he had been distracted by the screams of the young mother in the meat department. He cursed himself for not finishing off that eyewitness when he'd had the chance. Just in case she was too stupid to have escaped when he was busy in other parts of the supermarket, he ran toward her register.

Jennifer Weitz was indeed still cowering beneath her work area. The nineteen-year-old had wrapped herself into a fetal position and was trembling as she had been throughout the ordeal. That trembling had ceased intermittently during the few minutes since the event began. Each time a shot was fired, her muscles locked up for an instant before the shaking reasserted itself. Jennifer heard loud footsteps pounding rapidly toward her location and hadn't a doubt in her mind as to what would happen when they reached her. Finally, she bolted and ran toward the exit. She leaped over the body of the customer with as much grace and determination as a gazelle trying to outrun a lion.

Faleski rounded the corner from the aisle in which he had dispatched the elderly lady. The combination of his speed and the leather soles of his shoes caused him to lose his balance. He dropped into a three-point stance, using his free hand to stabilize himself while his gun hand aimed the pistol in the general direction of the fleeing clerk. Everything seemed to happen at once as he got back to his feet. A speeding police cruiser skidded to a halt just outside the glass front of the supermarket. The would-be vigilante vaulted out of his car and gestured wildly in his direction. The automatic door began swinging open and was assisted by the terrified clerk. He snapped off a single shot at her before scrambling toward the rear of the store.

Jennifer Weitz felt the movement of her hair as the round pushed it aside before penetrating the glass door. She ran past the police officer who was running at top speed toward the rear of the store and a few seconds later collided into his partner who headed toward the front entrance. Neither one of them fell. The cop helped the opening door just as she had done. His face was a study in concentration as he dashed toward the rear of the store with his pistol in hand. The blind terror prompted Jennifer to run right past her car in the parking lot and continue down the nearest sidewalk.

Before Faleski charged through the swinging doors into the stockroom at the rear of the supermarket, he heard the approaching cop chasing after him. The gunman sprinted to the door that led to the loading dock, knowing it may or may not be locked, and was filled with gratitude when he opened it and emerged onto the rear platform.

"Freeze! Drop your gun!" Faleski looked down at the policeman who was still running through the back lot after rounding the side of the building. The law officer turned himself into a stationary target, and Ray Faleski wasted no time in shooting him twice in the chest. Hearing those two shots as he reached the door to the loading dock, the partner of the man who had been hit emerged through the door with less caution than he knew he should have used. Faleski turned his weapon on his newest adversary, but was shot repeatedly by the officer whose protective vest had kept him alive.

As the two men bent over the killer, they were both certain he would be dead long before medical help arrived. Nevertheless, the cop who had not been shot made the call for that medical assistance. The other one used his bare hand to apply pressure to the wound that was bleeding the most profusely. But since that particular round had severed an artery in Ray Faleski's neck, he bled out and was not able to survive.

This was only her third visit to the health club, and Debra Dunn still felt a little self-conscious about being there. As she walked briskly on the treadmill she looked around the huge room at some of the other health-conscious people. Since it was late morning on a Monday, she didn't have all that many of them to check out. Only two other women and three men were availing themselves of the exercise equipment. She noted that all five of them had reached retirement age. No doubt most of the club's members who were around her age and younger were hard at work—or at least at work. Debra herself had the luxury of working at home and could schedule her trips to the health club when it was less crowded. Her first foray into the world of fitness had taken place on a Saturday. Huge mistake. Not only was it difficult to find any empty pieces of equipment, there were so many women flitting about who were almost half her age.

Not that she considered herself to be over the hill at thirty-six, but she wasn't going to be here among those wispy young women on purpose. She grinned as she thought of how the health-club manager, Carl Manning, had flexed and strutted for those adoring nymphets.

The hypnotic rhythm of walking on the belt of the treadmill made it easy for Debra to think about other things as she continued to perspire. In many ways, the past few months had been pleasantly fulfilling. Her syndicated column, "Debra Dunn's News Views," had been an instant success, which verified Jim Hopkin's assessment of her talent. She'd had a number of phone calls from him since he'd sold the newspaper and retired to Florida. He often invited both her and her father to visit him and his wife in Florida, which they both talked about doing at some point. But most of their conversations dealt with her new career and how happy he was for her. Hopkins sometimes teased her by asking her how often her new boss, Geoffrey Billings, hit on her. The millionaire who owned the newspaper syndicate had three divorces under his belt, and had a reputation for dating younger women. Jim Hopkins pretended not to be convinced by Debra's protestations that her relationship with Billings had a prayer—at least on her part—of being anything but business.

When Carl Manning entered the room and stood there surveying his domain, Debra knew he'd immediately head back to his office since there were no young women around to impress. When his eyes settled on her and he began walking in her direction, she groaned inwardly. She may be a lot younger than the other women in the room, but there was no way she was going to feed his ego and fawn all over him. He could damn well wait until his hard-body harem showed up later in the day, she thought. She turned off the motor on the treadmill and then stepped off the machine. After retrieving her cell phone from the control panel, she picked up her towel and headed for the ladies' locker room.

"Hi, I haven't had the chance to speak with since you've joined the club," Carl said as he gave her a smile which displayed teeth made to look even whiter due to his use of the club's tanning beds. "I'm the manager, Carl Manning." Debra had no choice but to shake his outstretched hand. She did have the choice not to admire the sculptured muscles that rippled during the handshake, but didn't seem quite able to take that option. Debra also couldn't help comparing his toned body with the slightly pudgy one of her ex-husband. Mentally berating herself for those unbidden thoughts, she decided to get this encounter over as quickly as possible.

"I recall seeing you here on a Saturday right after I joined. I'm Debra Dunn."

"Yes you are," he said, "and I'm one of your biggest fans. I read your column every day." He flashed that smile again, but this time she didn't find it offensive as she had before. The man hadn't approached her to stroke his ego; he was a reader who enjoyed her work. "Even though I wasn't the one who signed you up and showed you our facilities, I'd be more than willing to assist you in achieving your goals." He looked at her body in a manner that in any other surroundings might have been interpreted as lascivious. "You surely don't need to lose any weight, so I'm assuming you just want to tweak your tone a bit."

"Well now. Aren't you the flatterer," she said.

"I've been called worse," he admitted. "But I'm being totally honest."

"So you are a faithful reader, plus you honestly believe a woman my age doesn't need to shed a few pounds. Come now, Carl, I've already signed a contract for the year. There's no need to sweet talk me like I've seen you do with the teenyboppers and twenty-somethings."

He laughed. "Sounds like you were doing more observing than exercising when you here on Saturday. But then I guess that's what makes you such a good reporter. Truth is, trying to charm the clientele to keep them coming back for more is part of my job description."

"And you do it very well," she told him. "If I were ten years younger I very possibly would be standing here right now myself with my heart all aflutter."

"Give me a break. What are you, all of twenty-seven or twenty-eight?" Now he was carefully assessing her face instead of her body.

"No, you give *me* a break. You know darn well from reading those three little spaces for date of birth on my contract that I'm thirty-six. Your little charade is well-performed, but serves no useful purpose that I can think of." She made this announcement totally without rancor.

"Hey, Debra, I read your column because I like it, but reading all of the contracts would be more than a little boring. Sorry if I insulted you because I thought you were younger." The deep blue eyes were guileless as they looked directly into hers.

"Okay then," she said. "I guess I should just take my shower and then go home and think about how lucky I am to look eight or nine years younger than my chronological age."

Carl looked at the hint of a smile that she wore, and said, "You know, I can't tell if you're making fun of me or of yourself."

"Does it matter?" she asked. Now the smile was more than a hint.

"Um, I guess it shouldn't. But it might if you'd agree to go out with me sometime."

"Me go out with you?" She was genuinely surprised and her expression showed it. "Oh, that wouldn't be a very good idea. You may or may not have read my age on the contract before telling me I look younger, but it's easy to see that you are nine or ten years younger than I am. How foolish a woman would I have to be to think that dating you could turn into something?"

"I'm twenty-eight—only eight years your junior. And don't stand there and tell me that relationships with much wider age differences don't work out, because you know they do. Another thing, you and I would have a leg up on it because we have so many things in common."

Debra wiped some perspiration from her face and then flipped her towel onto her shoulder. Her curiosity piqued, she couldn't resist asking, "This should be interesting. Maybe I can do a column on May-December romances. What in the world do you and I have in common?"

"For starters, both of us are simply blown away by what a talented writer you are." In spite of herself, she giggled and, at that moment, she did indeed feel much younger than thirty-six. "And then there's the fact that we're both into physical fitness." Now it was Debra who wondered if she was being made fun of. "What about this?" He took her arm and gently turned her to face one of the floor-to-ceiling mirrors that lined the wall behind her. "If you and I don't look like two people who should be dating, I don't know who does. And finally—well, maybe not finally—but this is the last thing I'm going to mention now, I absolutely get off on helping people get into better physical shape, both here in the club and at home training sessions. I feel it was what I was destined to do. Ah, but you, Debra Dunn, you go into the homes of countless people around the country by means of your column. You not only go into their homes, but you also go into their minds and hearts. Your words tweak their emotions instead of their bodies, and help them to gain more insight into the emotions of others as well as the events that make up the news every day. Do you have any idea how good it would make me feel to have the opportunity to spend time with a person like you who gives so much to so many?"

They had both been looking at each other's images in the mirror as he had spoken, but now turned once again to face one another. She looked up into his face and said, "Wow."

"Was that a good 'wow' or a bad 'wow'?" he asked.

"I'm thinking I should call my boss and tell him to offer you a contract to write for his syndicate."

He grinned. "I'm a reader, not a writer. Haven't you been listening to me?"

"Oh, I've been listening all right. I don't know about you, but my schedule is completely open. When would you like to go out?" she asked.

"The sooner the better. Let's have dinner tonight."

"Yes, let's do that," she said. She smiled. "You already have my address and phone number on file. Did you want to pick me up at home, or would you prefer to meet at a restaurant?"

"Even though it's old-fashioned, I'd rather drive you to a restaurant. How about around seven?"

"I'll be looking forward to it, Carl."

"So will I, Debra. I'm really glad you decided to join the club and—"

Her cell phone warbled. "Excuse me," she said to him before she flipped it open. "Hello." She frowned. "No, I hadn't heard anything about it. I'm at a health club at the moment and haven't listened to the news since breakfast. What are the details?" Carl watched Debra's expression darken as she listened in silence. She interrupted her silence with a gasp and a moment later, asked, "What about the gunman? I see." Again she fell silent as she listened. "Definitely. I'll go home right now, pack a bag, take a quick shower and start driving. No, that would no doubt take much longer. Of course, I'll send it to you the minute I finish it. Yes, I'm sorry too. I'll be in touch. Good-bye."

As soon as she broke the connection, Carl said, "What was that all about? I heard you mention a gunman and that you're going to pack a bag and hit the road. You're not going to be doing anything dangerous, are you?"

"The only dangerous part is that I'm going to have to cancel our plans to have dinner tonight. I will admit that I was really looking forward to it. There was another mass murder. This one happened this morning in a supermarket in Chicago. The gunman killed seven people. Three of them were employed at the store and three others were shopping. The final victim was a six-month-old girl who was apparently not killed by a stray bullet—she was shot at close range, execution style."

"What a bastard! I hope they catch him and he gets the death penalty."

"He's already dead. Cops shot him as he tried to escape out the back. But that does nothing for the victims or their families. I am so sick and tired of all the violence in this country," she said. "Carl, I'm really sorry, but I have to leave. Maybe we can have that dinner sometime after I get back from Chicago."

"How long will you be away?"

"No way to tell. Depends on what happens there. I'm sure I won't be gone for more than a few days at the most. I'll call you as soon as I get back. Okay?"

"More than okay. Be careful, Debra." He put his hand on her upper arm and gently squeezed it.

Walking back and forth in her Chicago hotel room was not, Debra knew, what she should be doing. As she continued to pace, she occasionally glanced at her laptop computer that she had placed on the circular table. All of the emotions she wanted to change into words for her column were churning chaotically through her mind. The most powerful of those emotions was anger. She was also sad over what had happened in that supermarket—just like every other rational human being who knew of the tragedy—but it was her anger that dominated. How much longer, she wondered, would these senseless crimes continue?

Debra sat at the table and turned on the laptop. As soon as the cursor started blinking at the top of the screen, she stood and began pacing again. The information on the pages of her notebook as well as her mental notes demanded to make the transformation to the text that would be read by so many people. But she still wasn't ready to give in to that demand. The news of the supermarket slaughter was not received by the public with the degree of shock and notoriety it deserved because people had been desensitized to violence. And that desensitization would only deepen as these multiple slayings continued occurring. Debra wished that she had some magical, mystical way to stop it. Of course that was a wish that would never come true. All that she did have was the means to impart her thinking to her readers. She sighed as she sat once again. This time she began tapping the keys.

DEBRA DUNN'S NEWS VIEWS

It has happened yet again. This time the horror took place in a Value Plus supermarket on North Franklin Street in Chicago. On this occasion, the murder victims included three employees, three shoppers, and one six-month-old baby girl. The killer, twenty-eight-year-old Raymond Faleski, attempted to make good his escape by shooting a police officer twice in the chest. That officer's vest saved his life and allowed him to return fire. Faleski died on the loading dock of the supermarket.

The gunman had been the live-in boyfriend of twenty-two year-old Laura Porter. She had been beaten by him after telling him to leave her apartment according to one of the supermarket employees. This same source said that Laura had been trying to help Faleski get his life back on track. He had a lengthy arrest record, but none of the arrests had been for murder. Laura Porter's kindheartedness was repaid by her boyfriend with two rounds in her chest from a 9-mm semi-automatic pistol.

The manager of the supermarket, Ted Giroud, had recently fired Faleski for stealing substantial quantities of expensive food items. Mr. Giroud died after being hit with three shots from Faleski's weapon.

The final employee to lose his life was butcher, Vito Franconi. Mr. Franconi died a hero's death in a vain attempt to save the lives of others. He was found with a meat cleaver near his hand. The man's body was not in the cooler where he cut meat, but in an aisle next to the bodies of two other victims.

Although the spokesperson for the Chicago Police Department has yet to release the names of the four other victims, it is known that the women's ages were 21, 48 and 89. The forty-eight-year-old was gunned down as she tried to run out through the front door. The elderly lady was in the process of putting cans of cat food into her shopping cart when she was murdered. Police found the body of the young mother on the floor next to the shopping cart that held her slain baby. It doesn't take a master detective to come to the conclusion that the shoppers were killed to prevent the shooter's identification had his escape been successful. Also, the countless previous incidents of domestic and workplace violence tell us why the girlfriend and the store manager were murdered. The brave butcher died in a kill-or-be-killed situation. But the brutal and senseless execution of that baby girl angers me far beyond any words I can call upon.

How much longer will this country's politicians cower before the mighty gun lobby and that sizable segment of the population that condones the widespread ownership and use of weapons? The United States of America has such a long history of well-deserved pride for doing the right thing within our borders and around the world. But how much longer can that pride be maintained if USA continues to also stand for the Unlimited Slaughter of Americans?

Debra sent the finished column through the phone lines on its electronic journey to her syndication's headquarters. As always, she stored a copy and then closed the laptop. She got up from the table and looked out at the lights from the many buildings visible through the window. Knowing that in the rooms behind many of those windows there were people enjoying the companionship of one another. Whether they were friends, families, lovers, or merely acquaintances was immaterial. What mattered was that they were not alone. In spite of herself, Debra wondered what her former husband was doing at this very moment. Yes, he had cheated on her. And it was also true that she admitted to herself that her dedication to her job at the *Parkerton Examiner* had been at least partly to blame for Patrick having felt that he hadn't received enough of her attention during their marriage. But she had never thought he'd felt unloved until she learned of his affair.

She looked down at the traffic far below and wondered how many of those taxis and private vehicles carried couples to or from restaurants, theaters and dance clubs. Inevitably, this brought to mind her encounter earlier in the day with Carl Manning. They weren't even close to being categorized as a couple, but there definitely had been chemistry between them— of that she was positive. If only they had been out a few times by now, she'd have no reservations about picking up the phone and calling him to unload her anger and sadness that the day's interviews had instilled in her. But they had no history, so she couldn't do that.

Debra walked to the side of the window and closed the drapes. She'd had enough of that evocative view for one night. After plumping up two of the pillows on end at the headboard, she sat on the bed and leaned her back against them. Picking up the phone from the stand, she quickly punched a series of numbers. It was answered after the first ring and the familiar sound of his voice had her feeling better even before she responded.

"Hi, Dad. I just wanted to let you know that I'm okay," she said. She chuckled. "Were you sitting with the phone on your lap?"

"Not quite. But I was hoping you'd call to let me know how you're doing. How okay are you?"

"To be honest, I've had a lot better days than this one," she admitted.

"No doubt. As soon as I read your note when I got home from work, I started to worry about you."

"I would have driven by your route to find you and let you know what I was going to be doing, but that would only have started your worrying a few hours sooner."

"You know me so well. How bad was it up there today, Deb?"

"I suppose it could have been worse, but it was bad enough. I was able to talk with the partner of the officer who was shot. I wasn't able to really use anything he said, at least not yet, but what came across so strongly was how worried he was about his partner. It was his partner who had fired all of the rounds at the killer, so the guy I talked to was hoping that the counseling would help his buddy deal with the emotional trauma of taking a life."

"Yeah, that has to be rough," Bill Overfield said.

"And when the cashier, Jenny Weitz, was telling me about Laura Porter confiding in her that morning about her breakup with Faleski, the poor kid broke down. I felt like a ghoul for making her relive the whole incident all over again so soon."

"Well, I'm not going to sit here and tell you that you were only doing your job, so you shouldn't feel that way. I know how closely you identify with the people you talk with who have had terrible experiences. I remember how you've mentioned to me that you could never do TV news because you'd probably end of bawling too often when doing sad interviews. I bet that happened with this girl today, didn't it, sweetie?"

"As a matter of fact, no, it didn't. I was just too mad to cry. I simply can't stop thinking about that murdered baby. I feel so frustrated because this senseless violence keeps happening over and over and no one seems to be able to do anything to stop it. Before I started writing my column tonight, I was feeling so guilty because I have this unbelievable opportunity of a syndicated column to get my point across to so many people, but I know it's not going to end up doing one bit of good. The guns will always be out there, the politicians will always be ineffective, and people will always be dying needlessly."

After remaining silent for a moment, Bill said, "Debra, I know I'm not an expert like your former boss, but I do know that if Jim heard what you've just told me, he would say that you *are* doing a lot of good with your writing. You told me yourself that your new boss is so pleased with how more and more newspapers are signing on to carry you."

"I know. And, believe me, I'm grateful that people like to read what I write. But what I'm saying is that I wish that I could make my readers want to go out and actually *do* something about the problem instead of just sitting there sipping their morning coffee and commiserating with the victims of violence."

"Well, maybe commiserating is the forerunner of taking action," he said. "Wouldn't it be something if one of your dedicated readers gets so fired up one of these days and starts some sort of organization that actually starts to turn things around in this country? He or she would be like the exact opposite of that yahoo over in Thomasville, Illinois, who started GUN. It's not bad enough that his organization spouts how wonderful guns are, he also owns a factory that manufactures them."

"Ironic that you should mention him. The pistol that Faleski used to murder all of those people was made at Ryan Cordell's factory," she said. "I wonder how well he's going to sleep tonight."

"Probably a lot better than you are," her father said. "And without a doubt better than the family members of all the victims."

"I'm sure you're right, Dad. But you've just given me a great idea. Maybe I've been going about this the wrong way. Instead of trying to prick the consciences of the politicians and the public, I should be writing about the people like Cordell— people who either own the companies that make guns or who own stock in the larger companies." She was starting to get excited and could feel goose pimples forming on her arms. "I certainly can't do anything to make those poor families feel any better, but I sure as hell can make Ryan Cordell and everybody like him feel worse. Dad, as soon as I get home I'm going to give you a great big hug for giving me this idea."

He laughed. "I'll hold you to that promise, Deb. But you may run into a lot of flack from your boss if you start waging an all-out war on the firearms industry. You know how powerful those people are."

"I don't care," she said adamantly. "If Geoffrey Billings decides to fire me, let him. I'd rather go back to working for another small-town paper than back down from this. Come to think of it, I'd rather *deliver* papers in a small town before I back down."

Once again he laughed, but it was only because of his daughter's enthusiasm. "Debra Dunn throwing newspapers on people's porches with her baseball cap on backwards. Wouldn't the tabloids love to print that picture?"

Now he had her laughing. "You can take the picture yourself and sell it to them if it comes to that," she told him.

"Me selling you out to the tabloids is one thing you'll never have to worry about."

"That's good to know," she said, "especially because I'm going to be doing something in the near future that I probably shouldn't."

"Oh? And what scandalous activity will that be? Or would you rather see the shocked look on my face when I read the juicy story about you?"

"I've accepted a dinner invitation from a man who is only twenty-eight."

"My daughter a certified cradle robber. Hard to believe. I'm shocked to the core. Debra, the guy is barely out of his teens. Does he even shave yet?"

"Now I know why you're a letter carrier instead of a comedian," she said. "But it doesn't feel very funny to me."

"Oh, come on, Deb. An eight-year difference is no big deal. The worst that could happen would be if your friends tease you a little bit."

"I'm not worried about what my friends might say."

"Then who are you worried about? I hope you don't think your readers would care about such an insignificant and personal matter."

"No. I'm concerned that you will think I'm being foolish," she admitted.

"Me? Why in the world would you think that?" He looked surprised and more than a little puzzled.

"Because of my ex-husband."

"Because of him? Pat is a year older than you, Deb. You've really lost me here."

"Pat left me for a woman who was only twenty-three, Dad."

"Oh, okay. So it should follow that I would think you would be trying to somehow get back at your ex by dating a man who is eight-years younger than you. Gotcha. I'm glad I get paid to contend with bad weather, bad dogs, and a heavy mailbag instead of trying to figure out the convoluted logic of women." He chuckled. "Honey, if you start dating this guy and Pat somehow got wind of it, he might get more jealous than if the guy was his own age, but all that matters to me is that you're happy. If he's a decent guy that treats you right, I say go for it."

"I had already agreed to see him tonight just before I got the call from Geoff to come here to Chicago. I told Carl we'd get together as soon as I finish up here and come back home."

"I can tell by your voice that you're really looking forward to it. How'd you meet him?"

"He's the manager of the health club."

"Uh oh."

"Uh oh? What's that supposed to mean?" she asked.

"Only that most of the guys that work in those places are loaded with muscles, so I won't be able to intimidate him like I used to do to the boys when you first started dating."

She laughed. "You're too nice a guy to intimidate anybody. Even my pimply-faced dates way back then used to like you."

He ignored the compliment. "So as well as being toned, is this Carl good-looking?"

"Is he ever," she said.

"Well then, Debra. You can't wait to see the guy, he has a steady job, and you just got your father's blessing. Maybe in a year or so we'll have a little weightlifter running around the house."

"I think you might want to let me at least have my first dinner with the man before you start anticipating any grandchildren."

"Okay, Deb." He waited for a few seconds before saying, "But eat fast. I'm not getting any younger."

"That's right, grandpa, you'll be all of fifty-five on your next birthday." As soon as she said it, she wished she hadn't. Although her father had stopped talking about his plans to retire on that birthday as soon as his wife had died, Debra knew that his former plans to start doing some traveling with her mother were not forgotten.

"You know what that reminds me of?" he asked. His voice didn't sound suddenly sad or anything, but she still felt a lump starting to form in her throat. I'm sorry, Dad, she thought. "You are twice as old right now as I was when you were born. And yet you don't hear me going around teasing you about your age and not giving me any grandchildren yet. Oops, that's right. You just told me I'm such a nice guy. Maybe I should quit while I'm ahead." His voice was cheerful with the bantering; her worries about the tie-in with the loss of his wife and his upcoming birthday had been groundless.

"All I can say, Mister William Overfield, is that my biological clock is ticking just as fast as your heart would be beating if I ever am lucky enough to present you with a grandchild. How about this? If nothing materializes between Carl and me, I'll use my column as a forum to search for a husband. Only problem is, I'd have to find one pretty fast, because Billings would fire my butt if I pulled a stunt like that. Maybe I should just hang up and phone Carl Manning right now and tell him how much my father and I would like to see me married and pregnant. I bet he would leave town even faster than Pat did." She started laughing at the thought.

"Debra, I miss your mother so much." Her laughing immediately ceased. "I always thought she would be here with me when you had babies and to watch them grow up." The lump in her throat returned with a vengeance. "I loved her from the minute I met her when we were both in the seventh grade. Waiting until we were eighteen to get married seemed like forever to us." Debra kept the receiver against her ear but twisted the mouthpiece above her head as she cried as quietly as she could. "When she died, I don't . . . I don't think I could have gotten through it if you hadn't been with me." He tried to stifle a sob, but could not. Since they were now both openly crying, she twisted the mouthpiece back where it belonged.

After a few minutes of companionable sobbing, she was able to say, "Daddy, I miss her so much, too."

He managed to control his grief enough to say, "It just was so unfair. How could God allow her to die so young? Your mother was so good to me, and to you, and to everyone she knew. Towards the end, I used to go down into my workshop every night, get on my knees, and beg God to take her cancer away and give it to me." She let out a ragged sob when she heard that. "Oh, Debra, I'm so sorry. You have all of that terrible stuff to contend with right now for your column, and I'm doing this to you. I truly didn't mean to; it just came out."

"Daddy, it's all right. Really it is. I think we both have to just try our best to be as happy as we can. Maybe Carl and I will fall in love; maybe we won't. But the thing is, I don't want to go for the rest of life without someone just because Pat didn't love me enough to stay with me. And, Dad, I probably don't have any right to say this to you, especially not at this moment, but I honestly think that you should start looking for someone to be with." She waited to get his reaction, and when he didn't respond, she said, "Please don't be mad because I said that."

"Honey, of course I'm not mad. But I have nothing left inside to give any other woman. So it wouldn't be fair for me to pretend that I did. You can understand that, can't you?"

"I *do* understand how much you loved Mom—how much you'll always love her, but you should ask yourself what you would have wanted for her if God had let her live and taken you instead. Will you at least think about that?"

As he drove home from his factory, Ryan Cordell looked at the familiar homes and businesses and thought how fortunate he was to be living the American dream. To the best of his knowledge, he was Thomasville's wealthiest citizen; certainly the town's most visible millionaire. Who knew how many low-profile millionaires might be enjoying their wealth behind closed doors? But Ryan was not a man who chose to flaunt his good fortune. His sizable holding in the local TV outlet was known to only a handful of individuals. When he built the skating rink, however, a good deal of publicity had been lavished on the project from start to finish. It was he, and not his formerly-famous wife, who had chosen the fanciful name of Ice Dream for the rink. He had told Elaine that the name might just inspire other young skaters as well as Caitlin to follow their dreams of excelling in the world of competitive or professional skating. Caitlin herself liked the name because it sounded so much like ice cream.

Ryan's first and foremost business passion, however, was devoted to the Cordell Firearms Company. Granted, the organization for firearms proponents was a close second insofar as his time and attention were concerned, but the factory he'd inherited from his father would never be surpassed. He tried his very best to emulate his father's dedication to turning out superior products, and the brisk sales across the country and around the world attested to his success. Cordell weapons were appreciated by all who used them. The painstaking craftsmanship that went into each firearm guaranteed that it would function flawlessly when discharged. Ryan was understandably pleased by his collection of letters from satisfied customers praising the weapons. He especially appreciated the reports of lives being saved when private citizens or police officers employed Cordell weapons to get the best of criminals. Many a night he drifted off to sleep while contemplating the praiseworthy role that he and his employees played in those happy endings.

When he got within sight of his home, Ryan pressed the button of the garage door opener and then turned into the driveway. He had also inherited the ten-room house from his father and had no desire to build anything larger and more ostentatious. Both he and his wife were more interested in doing things with each other and their children than in impressing others with an expensive mansion. He had been spending more time with Luke since he had some exercise equipment installed in a basement room, but he was quite sure that his son wouldn't be bulking up anytime soon. Nevertheless, it was a worthwhile bonding experience for them, and he never minded when Luke often cut short the sessions to get back to his beloved books.

Ryan was whistling cheerfully as he walked through the doorway between the garage and the house. "You're not going to be so happy when you see this," his wife said as he entered the living room. He stopped whistling but kept walking until he reached the sofa and sat next to her. "I can't believe what this bitch wrote about you in the paper," Elaine said as she looked up at him from the newspaper she'd been reading.

"Some woman wrote a nasty letter to the editor? Is she one of my employees at the factory or the skating rink?" He looked puzzled as he tried to figure out which woman he might have offended in the recent past.

Elaine handed him the paper. "No. It's that Debra Dunn who both of us used to think was such a great writer."

"Debra Dunn *is* a great writer," he said as he took the newspaper. "And she is about as far from being a bitch as any woman I've ever met. What in the world did she write about me?" He held the paper open and spotted her column.

DEBRA DUNN'S NEWS VIEWS

I'll be leaving Chicago tomorrow. I'll be driving home to be with my family, my friends, and to continue on with my career. Gina Booker and her daughter, Jessica, will also be leaving Chicago tomorrow. The difference is that I'll be in my car and they'll be in a hearse. My work in Chicago will be finished; their work on earth has finished. Or has it?

After finding out that Gina and Jessica, two of the seven people gunned down in the Value Plus supermarket massacre, were killed by shots fired from a 9-mm semi-automatic pistol manufactured by the Cordell Firearms Company, I decided to check into that company. Unlike many of the factories that saturate our society with deadly weapons on a daily basis, this company is owned by a single person. Ryan Cordell inherited the company from his father and built it into the successful operation that it is today. One can't help but wonder how many other innocent people have died after being shot by a Cordell weapon over the years. We'll probably never know, because shooting deaths coming one or two at a time are hardly newsworthy in this country.

The aforementioned Mr. Cordell was not content to rest on his laurels after doing his part to supply our nation's criminals with the means to cowardly execute helpless men, women and children. Ryan Cordell also founded an organization to champion the cause of gun-toting Neanderthals in this country. GUN may be a not-for-profit organization, but its influence with members of Congress and lawmakers in every state in the union certainly helps to increase the profits of the Cordell Firearms Company as well as every other weapons manufacturer.

My guess is that a person like Ryan Cordell is extremely busy making deadly weapons as well as seeing to it that their sale and use is restricted as little as possible. Those pursuits must be quite time-consuming, so I doubt he has the time—not to mention the inclination—to read a column such as mine. So if any of you reading this *do* have a spare minute or two, please get in touch with Mr. Cordell for me and extend this invitation. I will be attending the funeral of Gina and Jessica Booker tomorrow morning to let my readers know what it feels like to say good-bye too soon to those two innocent victims. Please ask Ryan Cordell if he has the courage to stand by my side and see with his own eyes what one of those weapons he so proudly manufactures has done.

Ryan's hands were trembling as he placed the newspaper on the coffee table. He had lost most of the color from his face. "I can't believe this," he said as he turned toward his wife. "She has never viciously attacked anybody before now in one of her columns. Why did she decide to start with me? I certainly didn't murder any of those people. I'm only engaged in a legitimate business."

"Of course you are, Ryan." She felt like trying to get in touch with Debra Dunn and telling her just how good a man her husband truly is. "She's just trying to sensationalize your non-existent role in this because the gunman is dead. If he were in jail or on the loose, you can bet that she'd never have even thought of dragging you into this."

"I'm not too sure about that," he said. "I don't know if one of her bosses told her to do a character assassination on me or if this was her own idea. Either way, I hope she drops it before other bleeding hearts in the media jump on the bandwagon. Something like this could snowball and cause declining sales. The men and women at Cordell don't deserve to get laid off or lose their jobs because some nutcase reporter blames me for something that wasn't my fault."

"I know," she agreed. "Are you going to do anything about this?"

"Like what?"

"Like calling your lawyers and asking if a lawsuit is viable."

"Definitely not. That would only play into her hands and encourage her to draw it out. The best thing for me to do is simply ignore her and her column."

"You're probably right," Elaine said. "I know she was only challenging you to go to that funeral to play up to her readers, but at least its safe to say that even Debra Dunn doesn't have a big enough ego to believe that any of her faithful readers will try to get you to attend those services."

The phone rang before Ryan could comment. The man calling was from Tacoma, Washington, and Ryan didn't hang up on him until the caller started swearing at him for being a coward who would not attend the funeral in Chicago. Ryan Cordell took seven more hateful calls, which came in rapid succession, and then left the phone off the hook for the rest of the night.

As she parked her car in the parking lot of Parkerton's only health club, Debra wondered if she was making the right decision by coming here. Her father wouldn't be finished with his shift at the post office for another two hours, and she didn't want to be alone for that length of time. She had, in fact, not even stopped at their home after returning to Parkerton from Chicago. Feeling guilty because she was about to seek solace from a man she hadn't even been out with yet, she was, nevertheless, relieved to see that there weren't very many cars in the lot and felt he would have some time to give her.

Upon entering the huge room of the health club containing the multitude of exercise devices, she immediately spotted Carl Manning. He was standing next to a middle-aged man who was working out on a Bowflex. The perspiring customer made a comment, apparently funny, and the two men laughed. Carl's peripheral vision informed him of Debra's approach and he turned in her direction. His laughter instantly terminated. "Hey, Debra, you don't look too good. Is something wrong?"

"No . . . yes. Carl, can I talk with you for a minute if you're not too busy?"

"If he's ever too busy to talk to a beautiful woman, that would certainly be a first," the man working the Bowflex observed.

"You're just jealous because she didn't ask to talk to you," Carl said.

"No, I'm jealous because you're free as a bird and because my wife would take me for everything I own if I don't keep behaving myself."

"Amen, to that, brother. Let's go and talk in my office, Debra." They started off in that direction, but he veered off toward the juice bar. "I'm going to get us some drinks. You look like you could use something."

"I must look as bad as I feel," she said as she tagged along with him to the juice bar.

"Actually, you look great. But you appear to be a little tired, not to mention troubled." He blended various juices together in two large paper cups and handed one to her. She took a swallow and then another. "Good isn't it?" he asked. "That should help perk you up. Come on."

Once inside his office, he closed the door and sat near her in one of the two chairs on the visitors' side of his desk. He waited for a moment before saying, "I hope that you aren't here to tell me that you changed your mind about having dinner with me. I'm going to look even sadder than you if you have."

She managed a brief smile. "No, I'm still looking forward to that. I thought I would stop in for a few minutes because I felt we sort of got along well the other day and I just got back from Chicago to an empty house. I live with my dad—he's a widow—and I'm kind of upset over dealing with that whole business of the shootings and the funeral."

"I absolutely hate to go to funerals," he said.

"So do I," she said. "But I felt like I had to go to this one. I'm going to be writing as much as possible about all of the senseless violence in the country, and seeing that young mother lying in her coffin with her baby is an image that should keep me resolved about my crusade."

"Oh, Debra. You went to *that* funeral. No wonder you look the way you do."

"Carl, it broke my heart to see them. I don't think there was a single person in the room who didn't cry at one time or another. I love what I do for a living, but I can honestly say that attending those services was the worst thing I've had to face since I became a reporter." He watched her take another drink and saw that her eyes were still reddened from crying.

"Well, maybe a lot of people that read your columns about the criminals that commit these types of crimes will do something to at least cut down on them. I suppose you're going to campaign to get your readers to get in touch with the members of Congress to ask for stricter gun control laws."

"Actually, I'm going to blast the people who manufacture the guns, starting with the company that made the pistol used in this case."

"I see. I read the column about that Cordell guy, but I thought it was more or less a one-time thing."

"No way. I intend to keep after him and everyone like him as much as possible."

Carl frowned. "I know it's none of my business, but aren't you worried about getting fired. Those gun manufacturers and gun lobbies are powerful people with deep pockets, probably even deeper than your boss, Geoffrey Billings."

She had been in the process of lifting her cup to her lips, but stopped the motion and said, "That's a surprise. I'm sure most of my readers don't know and don't care that I work for his syndicate. Why do you?"

He blushed. "I sort of researched you on the Internet."

"You did? Should I be concerned? You're not some sort of combination health guru and stalker, are you?"

Carl grinned. "The only people I stalk are potential customers for the club. You would be totally safe in my company."

"That's good to know," she said and finished the remaining juice in her cup.

"Want some more?"

"Thanks, but no. I don't want to spoil my appetite," she said.

"Which presents me with the perfect opportunity to ask if tonight would be a good time to make good on our agreement to have dinner together." Her hesitation as well as her body language told him she was about to renege. "If the Chicago trip has left you wanting to postpone, I understand. But I hope you won't make me wait too long; I'm really looking forward to getting to know you better." The sincerity she saw in his expression touched her in a way she hadn't experienced for some time now.

"To be perfectly honest with you, Carl, I had been contemplating getting into my pajamas and robe and watching TV with my dad tonight. But if you don't mind a dinner companion who is admittedly not in a festive mood, I'll see you tonight."

"Perfect!" He smiled, "As you can see, I'm not very good at pretending to be cool and laid back. I guess that's why I never had any aspirations to be an actor. What you see is what you get with me."

"I'm sure I wouldn't have the desire or the patience to deal with an actor's ego, so maybe we should both be glad you're into physical fitness and managing a gym."

"Please, we never use the term gym these days. That's much too archaic."

"Not to mention much less expensive," she said.

"How true. But to better impress you, I'm also a personal trainer and a licensed masseur. So then, how impressed are you?"

"Very much so. Plus, I won't have to go home now and research you on the Internet." She smiled and got to her feet. "I guess this is normally the time when you would shake a person's hand and offer your thanks for another signing of a contract to join the club."

Carl stood as well. "That's exactly what I'd be doing if you had just signed up. But under the circumstances that brought you here today, I don't think a handshake would suffice." She wore a look of surprise as he quickly closed the gap between them and enfolded her in a hug. Her surprise was evidenced by her rigidity, but that rapidly dissipated. "I'm sorry you had such a bad time of it on your assignment, Deb." She relaxed even more after he said that. Leaning her cheek against his chest felt like the most natural thing she'd ever done. "So can I pick you up at seven for dinner tonight?"

"Um hmm," she murmured and nodded her head a few times without moving it away from his body. She wished she could stay right where she was until seven. Debra also wished that the evening would go well and be followed by a succession of others. Since he seemed to be willing to hold her for as long as she needed to be held, Debra was the one to back away from the embrace. But when he kept one arm around her and touched her cheek with his other hand, she knew she was about to be kissed and molded her body against his once again.

CHAPTER FOUR

Sitting behind the desk in his office usually made Ryan Cordell feel content and proud. Contentment and pride were absent from his list of emotions as he finished reading Debra Dunn's newspaper column. He left the newspaper lying on his desk and got up to walk to the window. Looking out at the well-kept lawn, shrubbery and the woods beyond, Ryan reflected upon how much more substantial the factory had become since he had helped out here when still a boy. Back then, only a handful of employees produced rifles that were used for hunting large and small game as well for target shooting. It was only after he had taken over the business that Cordell Firearms began to manufacture handguns. What he had to be extremely careful to avoid, would be allowing misguided media people like Debra Dunn to make him feel guilty about his place in society. The protection that his weapons provided to ordinary people far outweighed the few incidents of violence like the latest in Chicago. Knowing he was right was one thing, but the haunting words of her column beckoned him back to his desk to read it again.

DEBRA DUNN'S NEWS VIEWS

The funeral home where services were held for Gina Booker and her six-month-old daughter, Jessica, was crowded. In fact, the funeral director told me that more mourners had attended than even those services for police officers, firefighters, and local politicians that had been held there over the years. As I had stood there looking down at the bodies of the young mother and her baby, those words I had just heard from the funeral director overshadowed the background noise of sobbing and muted conversations. That baby girl had never arrested any criminals, had never fought any fires, had never won any elections. And yet, it was safe to assume that the overwhelming number of strangers who paused briefly to look into the coffin and pray were there because of little Jessica.

Gina Booker was dressed for eternity in an orchid nightgown. Maybe it was my imagination, but the young mother's mouth appeared to show the hint of a smile. We all know that there are crude references made as to the likely reasons for a person to die with a smile, but being gunned down by a total stranger in a local supermarket isn't one of them. No, if indeed my eyes were not deceiving me, Gina would be smiling forever because her only child was nestled in her left arm close to her heart. Jessica was dressed in a pink nightgown. This nightgown featured no hearts, or roses, or teddy bears embroidered into it—the angelic face of the little girl was all of the ornamentation needed. What was needed, however, was the pretty pink headband to cover the entrance wound of the bullet that ended Jessica's life.

Whether sitting or standing, Matthew Booker hardly ever took his eyes away from his wife and daughter where they lay just a few feet from him. Both his parents and his wife's parents were also there in the front row, but the agony of that young husband and father tore at my heart with a poignancy that will never be forgotten. Given the circumstances of the deaths, one might expect anger, naked rage, and even a desire for some type of revenge to show in his expressions. But that was not so. He looked confused and unimaginably sad.

Having mentioned some of the family members and others who were there, I'd like to briefly note that the manufacturer of the murder weapon chose to ignore my invitation to attend. Two of my readers had gotten in touch with me to let me know they had personally spoken with Ryan Cordell after reading my column, so it's not as if he had been unaware of my challenge. Of course, I wasn't in the least surprised. After all, Mr. Cordell has much more important things to do with his time. He has to make certain that the Cordell Firearms Company's production doesn't slow down; this country has many more innocent men, women and children slated for death by gunfire.

"Damn that woman!" Ryan shouted and slammed the side of his fist on the desk. The pictures and framed awards on the office walls were still rattling when his secretary buzzed. He sincerely hoped she wasn't about to ask if he was okay; Ryan was in no mood to be fawned over by a solicitous female at the moment. But all she asked was if he would see Bertram Dupont, the founding attorney of the law firm that handled most of the legal matters, both private and business, for Ryan Cordell.

The lawyer entered a few seconds after the secretary relayed her boss's approval of the unexpected visit. There could be no mistaking that Ryan's attorney was in anything but an angry mood as he strode to the desk with a newspaper clutched in his hand. After glancing down at the same paper that was opened to Debra Dunn's column, he deposited his newspaper on top of it with a resounding slap. "I see you've already read that load of crap!" he said. "That bitch really stepped over the line this time, Ryan."

In spite of his own foul mood, Ryan could not help chuckling. "Bert, I bet no one has ever accused you of holding back your emotions."

"I don't get paid to hold back my emotions of any other damn thing," he snarled.

"No, I suppose you don't," Ryan agreed.

"You're damn right I don't. The only question here," he swatted both papers but didn't pick either one up, "is how quickly can we file suit against her, the newspapers that printed this garbage, and the syndicate she works for."

Cordell looked up at the angry attorney and knew it would be best to choose his words carefully. "Bert, have a seat and we'll discuss this." Dupont's expression and body language made no secret of the fact that the last thing he wanted to do was allow himself to become placated. Reluctantly, he sat in one of the visitors' chairs. "Believe me, Bert, I'm at least as angry as you are about this." He, too, put his hand on the offensive newspapers, but in a restrained manner. "But I can't help wondering if a long, drawn-out lawsuit would be in the best interests of my company."

Bert Dupont bounced to his feet and started pacing briskly back and forth. "Come on, Ryan. We can't lay down and play dead with something like this. That's the *last* thing you want to do. That little weasel will keep yapping at your heels if we don't use the courts to shut her up." Dupont, who had a fringe of mostly-gray hair around his shiny bald head, was a full head shorter than Ryan, but had the brawny look of a street fighter. Having seen him in action in a number of courtroom appearances, Ryan was well aware of the man's ability to charm, energize, and intimidate juries. "If we sit back and do nothing, *that's* what could very well end up hurting your business, not to mention your organization and your reputation. How do you think the members of GUN would react if they perceive you as being whipped by this bleeding-heart reporter?" Once again he tapped the newspapers, but used much less force this time. He resumed his seat, but looked ready to start moving about the room again at the slightest provocation.

"I'm really not concerned with GUN members; my employees are the ones I'd be worried about if this thing gets out of hand."

"If? *If* it gets out of hand? Wake up, guy. That train has already pulled out of the station." Not surprisingly, Bert was once again on his feet. "Ryan, you've worked too damn hard to build this business up to let some flea-brained bimbo ruin it for both you and your employees. You just give me the word and I'll ram it so far up that bitch's ass that she'll never be able to sit down again to write any more lies about you."

"I think you just blew your chances to become this year's poster boy for political correctness," Ryan observed.

"Go ahead, make jokes, but it won't be so funny if your sales start slacking off and you have to give the ax to some of your employees." The attorney sat down. "Ryan, look," he said in a reasonable tone, "we both know I tend to come on pretty strong when I get riled up—that's the way I am. But this woman has me so pissed off because she's so far off the mark here. We can't let her paint you as some off-the-wall enabler of blood-thirsty criminals and get away with it. It just isn't fair."

"You're right, Bert. It isn't fair. But I guess I'm a bit more reluctant than you are to jump in with both feet here. What if we go to trial and the whole thing blows up in our faces? I realize that this Debra Dunn is using me personally to vent her anger and frustration on because I own this company. But if we turn around and use personal attacks on her, maybe that could turn into a can of worms we never should have opened. To me, she's only a name on a newspaper column. For all I know, she's some twenty-something youngster who got lucky and was taken under the wing of that Billings guy who owns the newspaper syndicate. Or what if she turns out to be some sweet old grandmother who has selected me as a villain for her last hurrah?"

"Anytime you want to enter combat, you have to know your enemy," the lawyer advised as he removed a small notebook from the inside pocket of his suit. "Debra Dunn is thirty-six. She lives with her father in his home in Parkerton, Indiana. Her mother is dead. Her husband, Patrick Dunn, left her for a young tramp who dumped his ass shortly thereafter. She worked for Jim Hopkins at the *Parkerton Examiner* from the time she graduated from college until he sold the paper a few months ago and retired to Florida. I suspect, but I'm not certain, that Hopkins landed her the job she holds now because he and the syndicate's owner, Geoffrey Billings, were college roommates and are still close friends. Her column is getting more popular even as we speak, with new newspapers signing up each week." He closed the tablet with an audible snap before putting it back into his pocket.

"I have to concede that you are thorough, Bert." Now it was Ryan who got to his feet. He, however, walked to stand and look out of the window instead of pacing. "As well as worrying about my employees, I also have to think about my wife and kids." He turned back to face his attorney before saying, "I don't want them to suffer needlessly if we get embroiled in a knock-down, drag-out fight. You have to remember, Bert, the attorneys you'd be up against would be bankrolled by the various newspapers as well as the syndicate. There'd be some deep pockets involved." Dupont started to say something, but the businessman cut him off with an upraised hand. "Don't get me wrong. I fully appreciate the fact that you can hold your own with any number of high-powered attorneys, Bert. It's just that I want to hold back for awhile to see if there's some other means of settling this."

"I don't follow you. Are you saying you'd want me to merely threaten a lawsuit by sending her a letter?"

"No. I'm wondering if it wouldn't be smarter for me to contact her and try to get her to understand that I'm not the demon she is making me out to be."

Bert got up and walked over to stand in front of Ryan. "Since you pay me for my advice, I feel justified in advising you that that would be useless. This woman is no pushover like Rebecca Sinclair who will swoon over your palpable charisma."

"Oh, not you, too. That's all I've heard from Elaine since that taping."

The lawyer chuckled. "I'm not surprised. But you have to bear in mind that this Dunn woman is a piranha out for blood—your blood."

"So it seems. But for the time being, I'm going to hold off on any court action and make an effort to talk with her. If that approach fails, we can consider filing a lawsuit."

"Oh, it will fail all right. There's no point in the two of us debating this issue any further right now. You just give me a call after she turns down your request to be reasonable and I'll get the ball rolling."

After Ryan thanked his attorney for his impromptu visit and his concern, they shook hands and Bert Dupont left the office. Ryan turned back to look at the peaceful scene outside his window.

As he sat and listened to his favorite teacher talk about the recent book the group had read, Luke Cordell was having a difficult time focusing on Jared Bernstein's words. This was only the second time that Cheri Morris had attended the extra-curricular session, but Luke's crush on her had him uncharacteristically distracted from his love of literature. With her addition to the group, the total came to only eleven, so there were plenty of extra seats available in the classroom. But both times she had sat right across from Luke, so his fourteen-year-old ego attached an awful lot of significance to that.

Luke's eyes were trained on the teacher, although his peripheral vision missed not a single movement made by Cheri. On those few occasions when he thought her head turned slightly in his direction, his heart raced with anticipation. He planned to talk with her for the first time in the hallway as soon as the session ended. There was a school dance scheduled in two weeks and he planned to ask her to go with him. The fact that he hadn't yet learned to dance did not dissuade him. Watching music videos in his locked bedroom had given him opportunities to perfect some moves. And if she did agree to go to the dance with him, he was absolutely certain that his mom would teach him to slow dance; he knew that mothers ate that kind of stuff up.

Since he had never been on a date before, Luke thought it might be advisable to see if she wanted to go to a movie or to hang out at the mall sometime before the dance. That way, he reasoned, they'd be more familiar with each other and therefore be more at ease around the other kids at the dance.

Luke was certain he had an excellent chance of dating her. When she made her first appearance last week, Jared Bernstein had introduced her to the group and mentioned that she had recently transferred to Thomasville High School and then he'd asked her to tell the others about herself. Cheri had said that her goal in life was to become an actress and that the guidance counselor had urged her to attend Mr. Bernstein's Friday afternoon sessions. His reasoning had been that because so

67

many movies had first been novels, this particular extra-curricular activity would be beneficial to her. Since his own aspirations dovetailed quite nicely with hers, Luke immediately thought he should attempt to get to know her. And then, when she disclosed that she hoped it wouldn't be too difficult to make friends in this new school, his heart soared with the knowledge of what kind of friend he would like to be to her.

Upon hearing her say that she was a sophomore instead of a member of his freshman class, he hoped that wouldn't mess up his plans. Even if she was a year or so older, she was easily a head shorter than he was, and thin enough to make his slight build a non-issue. Yes, he definitely had a good feeling about this.

Luke turned his head slightly in her direction. At that moment, Cheri took her eyes off the teacher, saw Luke looking at her, and smiled. To be sure, the smile was brief, and her attention immediately returned to Bernstein. But Luke's imagination went into overdrive. Instead of being content to picture the two of them having a good time at a movie or the dance, Luke was vividly portraying an image of an encounter with Cheri Morris in which he was assuring her that he could get her a starring role in the movie that was about to be made from his latest best-selling novel. In his fantasy, she looked up into his eyes with an expression that left no doubt in his mind as to how she would show her appreciation for his benevolence.

"And so Reggie definitely had a hidden agenda when she asked Kurt for that meeting. Why do you suppose that Kurt was so blind as to not know what it was? Luke, what do you think?" the teacher asked. "Luke?"

Luke's expression showed that he hadn't a clue as to what the question had been. "Uh . . . uh, I'm sorry, Mr. Bernstein. I guess my mind was wandering for a minute."

Jared Bernstein had caught the smile that Luke had received from Cheri. He said, "Yes, that happens to all of us now and then." The perceptive teacher could not resist the briefest of glances at Cheri before saying to Luke, "From the look on your face, wherever your wandering mind visited was certainly a happy place." It took all of Luke's willpower not to turn in Cheri's direction to see if she noticed how deeply he was blushing. Jared felt sorry for the sensitive boy, who also was one of his favorite students, and acted to end Luke's discomfort. "Tell you what, gang," he said as he looked at the wall clock, "I know we usually hang out until four, but I have a few things I have to do today, so we'll knock off early. See you all here next Friday."

It appeared that the students had things to do as well, judging from the way they hurried toward the door. The notable exception was Luke. He was every bit as perceptive as his teacher and was just about certain that the man somehow fathomed the reason for his embarrassment and that he had desperately needed to catch up with Cheri to ask her that all-important question. The boy started for the door, but hesitated and turned back to face the teacher. He felt like finding out if his instincts were correct and that Bernstein made up the story about having things to do so that Luke could pursue romance—it seemed important that a future author verify that type of hunch. When Jared saw Luke turn back toward him, he gave the boy a smile and a thumbs-up. Luke knew his instincts had been correct and smiled back at his favorite teacher before hurrying to catch up with Cheri in the hallway.

"Hey, Cheri, wait up. I want to talk to you," Luke called as he hastened toward her.

"You do?" she asked as she turned toward him after stopping short. One of the boys from the group had been right behind her, and he mumbled a quick apology after jostling her.

"Yeah, I sort of wanted to see if you would go with me to the dance that's coming up two weeks from tonight." He saw a subtle change in her expression, but couldn't figure out what it might mean. "And I wondered if maybe we could go to a movie or something before that to, you know, get to know each other a little better first." Now she was frowning. Luke didn't think that preceded any words he wanted to hear.

69

"Luke, I have a boyfriend." The frown was now replaced by a smile, but it was patronizing and Luke hated it.

"But . . . but I thought you said last week that you were looking for new friends. And I definitely remember Mr. Bernstein saying that you just transferred here."

"I did just transfer here. My mom and dad were recently divorced and my mother and I just moved here from Rossville. That was where I met my boyfriend, Dominic Pennoni. He's on the football team here; do you know him?"

"The Dominator is your boyfriend?" Luke said. Everybody in the high school knew of the huge lineman's reputation for hurting opposing players as well as bullying other teenage boys while not in uniform. Luke had a hard time picturing this petite girl who wanted to become an actress with a rough guy like Pennoni.

"So you do know him." She laughed. "I hate Dom's nickname, but I suspect that he loves it. I think it makes him feel invincible both on and off the field."

"I guess so." Luke swallowed hard.

"Anyway, Luke, thanks for asking me to the dance. It was sweet of you to want to help me make friends in my new school. But at least we'll get to see each other every Friday afternoon. By the way, I was really impressed last week when Mr. Bernstein mentioned the fact that you plan to write novels after you go to college."

Luke felt like a complete fool as he remembered his recent fantasy dealing with both their aspirations. How rapidly a romantic fantasy can fade when a brawny football player becomes part of the equation. It was a good time for Luke to try his hand at acting he felt as he said, "Yes, we future writers and actors should stick together." Great! He delivered the line as if his major crush on this beautiful girl wasn't making him feel as if this was the worst day of his life. "It will be nice to at least see you here on Fridays," he added, and then immediately cursed himself for sounding so pathetic and needy.

"Cheri, what's going on here?" Dom Pennoni demanded as he walked toward them. "Is this little geek bothering you?"

Luke looked at the towering hulk who stopped less than two feet away and glared down at him.

"No, Dom, he's not bothering me. He just asked me to go to the dance with him because he didn't know you were my boyfriend."

"He what?" Luke saw that the puzzlement in Dom's expression was indeed genuine.

"Dom, this is Luke Cordell. We're both members of Mr. Bernstein's literary group."

For a fraction of a second, Luke considered attempting to shake hands with the guy, but concluded that could end up with losing the mobility of his hand for days.

"Cordell? Are you related to the guy who owns the gun factory?" Dom asked.

"Ryan Cordell is my father," Luke said.

"He is? Well, listen to me, little rich boy. I don't care how much money you and your old man have, if I ever catch you trying to fool around with my girl again, you'll be sorry." Pennoni reached out and began backing Luke up toward the built-in lockers that lined the hallway by prodding his chest with his beefy index finger. He underscored each word with a powerful jab of his finger as he said, "Do you understand me, Mr. Puke Cordell?"

Right before Luke's back crashed into the metal lockers, Jared Bernstein walked out of his classroom. "Pennoni! What do you think you're doing?"

Dominic Pennoni's angry expression turned to surprise as his head swiveled toward the teacher. "Nothing. We were only talking." His statement was demonstrated to be false since his finger was still pressed against Luke's chest.

"In actuality, Mr. Pennoni, you have just physically assaulted one of your fellow students. Counting Luke, there were three witnesses to that assault. Are you aware that what you have just done could result in criminal charges, suspension

71

or expulsion, and last, but not least, the end of your high school football career? I don't know if you realize it or not, Dominic, but Luke's father owns the Cordell Firearms Company and is Thomasville's wealthiest citizen. If you think a man like that is going to let you get away with criminal behavior against his son, you've taken too many hits to the head in that barbaric sport of yours. As soon as I make a few phone calls, you may well be on your way to doing some serious prison time."

"But . . . but I was only tapping him a little." Pennoni finally realized his finger was still pinning Luke against the lockers and let his arm drop to his side. "It's not like I slugged him or anything."

"Not like the other guys you've been known to beat up on, you mean?"

"Yeah . . . I mean, no." Dom looked at his girlfriend for some much-needed help.

"Mr. Bernstein, Luke didn't know that Dom is my boyfriend and had asked me to go a dance and Dom got upset. Please give him another chance. He's really not a bad person. Please don't call the police and get him in trouble."

It appeared to Dom that the teacher was softening his stance, so he said, "Yeah, Mr. Bernstein, I just got a little upset."

Jared Bernstein ignored the football player. "You're really his girlfriend, Cheri?"

"We've been going together for more than a year now, Mr. Bernstein."

"I see."

Again Dom wasted no time in trying to capitalize on the teacher's apparent waffling. "Mr. Bernstein, I know I sometimes throw my weight around a little more than I should. If you just cut me some slack here, I promise I'll try really, really hard to control my temper better." He paused to listen and watch to see what effect his plea had on the man. Bernstein's demeanor didn't seem to change. Always being the toughest guy around made it extremely difficult for Dom to put his tail between his legs and beg, but if ever a situation called for swallowing that bitter pill, this was it. "Please, Mr. Bernstein, I have to keep playing football so I can get a college scholarship in order to make into the NFL someday. Like I said before, I *promise* you that I won't do more stupid stuff like this in the future. Please, please, man, give me another chance."

"I'll tell you what I'll do, Dominic. I *will* give you another chance to follow your football dreams, but only on two conditions."

The huge high school junior looked as if he had just been given a last-minute reprieve by a state governor concerning a crime much more serious than what he had done here. He was actually smiling as he said. "Anything. I'll do anything you say if you forget about this."

"Oh, none of us standing here today are ever going to forget about this. The first thing I want you to do is to agree to get therapy for anger management. I can set that up through the school system. I want there to be no more bullying of any more students by you simply because you're tougher than everyone else and can't control your temper."

"I'll do it," he readily agreed. "I'll save up any anger I might have for the opposing teams. What's the other thing I have to do?"

"The other condition has to do with Luke and his father. If the two of them decide not to bring charges against you, I won't press the matter."

Pennoni looked dumbfounded. "You mean my whole future depends on him giving me a break?" He looked at Luke, who was still leaning heavily against the lockers. "You know very well both him and his old man will never let me off the hook for pushing him around a little. I mean, look at the size of him; any judge will lock me up for the max if I get arrested. And you know that's true, Mr. Bernstein."

"What I know to be true, Mr. Pennoni, is that Luke here has dreams for his future just as well as you have for yours. He wants to write novels and, if I'm not mistaken, your fellow student here is at this very moment thinking how pivotal a

73

decision like the one he's about to make would be in any novel. However, this is not a work of fiction, this is real life. So I must admit, Dominic, I am every bit as curious as you are as to what Luke Cordell is going to decide."

Dom looked down at the face of the kid who was staring at the teacher. The football player felt like he was seconds away from embarrassing himself by vomiting. His whole career, his entire life, would depend on the words of a skinny nobody who had had the nerve to hit on his girlfriend. He began to perspire heavily as he tried to keep the impulse to throw up at bay as he waited for the words that would humiliate him in front of his girlfriend and send him to jail.

"Mr. Bernstein," Luke said, "my dad won't do anything about this, because I'm not going to tell him what happened. I should have known better in the first place than to think that a girl like Cheri would go out with a guy like me." He turned to Dom and held out his hand. "I honestly hope that you make it into the NFL someday." As Dominic took the offered hand and shook it, his upset stomach was no longer a problem, but the shock of what he heard overwhelmed him emotionally. He began to sob uncontrollably as he let go of Luke's hand and hurried to lean against the lockers for support.

"Mr. Bernstein, I'm going home," Luke said and started to walk away.

"Luke, thank you," Cheri said as she stopped his movement by holding his arm.

He looked down at her hand briefly and then into her eyes. He nodded and then said, "I'll see you back here next Friday."

Just before Luke turned the corner in the hallway, he glanced back to see that Jared Bernstein was looking at him. Cheri had Dominic turned away from the lockers and was hugging him as he continued to sob.

"How come you're home so early?" Luke asked his father as soon as he unlocked the front door and saw Ryan reading a newspaper in the living room. "A slow day at the factory?"

"No. I thought I'd knock off a little early and spend some time working out with you before we meet your mother and Caitlin for dinner." The Cordell family's Friday afternoon consisted of Elaine coaching Caitlin's skating session at Ice Dream and then going to one of the local restaurants with Ryan and Luke. "You up for a workout before we go to the rink?"

"I guess so," Luke replied with little enthusiasm. He had planned on coming home to an empty house and reading until dinnertime. That way he could try to forget the double humiliation of his first attempt at dating and then being manhandled by Cheri's boyfriend.

"You look kind of down," his father observed. "Did you have a problem in school today?"

If you only knew, Luke thought. But of course he couldn't divulge what had gone on in the hallway outside of Mr. Bernstein's classroom. Luke contented himself with the fact that his father would have approved of his noble act had he known. "No, Dad, no problems at school. I'll go throw on some sweats and we'll go see who can do more reps." He smiled to prove to his father that nothing was troubling him. Ryan was anything but convinced that his son was having no difficulty, but like any father of a fourteen-year-old boy in that difficult time of life, he had no choice but to accept his son's version of the truth.

Elaine watched her daughter with a practiced eye as Caitlin performed a flawless jump, landing it with the grace and sureness of a skater two or three times her age. It was easy to tell from Caitlin's expression that the six-year-old had no doubt whatsoever as to how well she had executed the jump. Still, she wanted verbal confirmation. "How was that one, Mom?" she asked as she glided to a stop next to Elaine.

"That one was so good that I wish we had it on tape so we could show your father," Elaine gushed as Caitlin looked up at her with undisguised admiration.

"That was one great jump, Caitlin," Ryan said enthusiastically as he and Luke walked toward them outside of the railing surrounding the ice.

"Yeah, at least you didn't fall on your butt," Luke said.

"You are *so* funny, Luke," Caitlin said as she skated to the male members of her family. "Mom thought it was pretty good too, Dad."

"Well then, if your mother agrees with me, I guess I know what I'm talking about."

Elaine skated toward them and Ryan leaned over the barrier and held his arms wide. She judged her speed expertly and landed softly against him. He kissed her lips briefly but continued hugging her. "What's all this about?" she asked. "Did you miss me that much today, or are you just hungrier than usual?" She consulted her watch. "You are earlier than usual."

"Oh, a little of one and a lot of the other," he teased. "I left the factory a bit earlier today. Luke and I spent some time working out afterward and here we are."

She looked at her son and then back at her husband. "Is something going on between you two? You guys weren't arguing about something or other, were you?"

"You gotta be kidding," Ryan said. "Didn't I tell you the other day that this guy is too lean and mean for me to pick on any more."

"Yeah, right," Luke said. "I'm going to play some video games until you guys are ready to leave."

He started to head for the game room. "Luke, you need some money?" his father asked.

"No. I have enough." He walked away.

"Are you sure there's nothing going on, Ryan? He just doesn't look right. And neither do you," Elaine said. Caitlin moved her feet in such a way as to skate backward and forward a few inches at a time while looking up at her parents.

"Caitlin, you can go out and practice for a few more minutes before we leave," Ryan said. "Show me what Mommy's been teaching you lately."

"Okay, Daddy." She smiled at him and then skated away. Her mother and father watched as she did some fancy footwork, then skated backwards for a moment, before turning around and doing another jump. This one wasn't timed correctly and with her landing foot in the wrong position, she ended up with her rear end bumping down on the ice. Caitlin was immediately back up and skating, and, as soon as she had enough momentum, she performed the jump flawlessly. After flashing a brilliant smile at her parents, she skated off to the far end of the rink. Elaine had turned her body to face the rink, but she leaned back against the barrier with Ryan's arm wrapped around her waist.

"I asked Luke if he'd had some sort of problem in school when he came home," Ryan said. "He wouldn't admit to anything, but you know how guys are. I'm sure he'll be fine. He's at a rough age now."

"Yes," Elaine agreed. "And what about you?"

"Oh, being forty-five is no picnic. You'll find out when you get there."

She ignored his attempt at humor. "It's that rotten Debra Dunn, isn't it? You're really letting her get to you. I wish she'd let up on you and pick on somebody else."

"As a matter of fact, I've pretty much decided to try to call her and see if she'll meet with me. Maybe I can convince her that she's being unreasonable with this little crusade of hers."

"I agree. And the sooner the better," Elaine said with conviction.

"You do? That's a surprise."

"Why should it be? What better way to show her what a decent man you are than to talk to her in person?"

"That's how I feel. I was under the misconception that you might go off on a jealousy tangent like you did before Rebecca Sinclair interviewed me," Ryan admitted.

"Rebecca Sinclair," she said in a desultory manner. "You can hardly compare that little sex kitten with a woman who's been around the block as many times as Debra Dunn."

Ryan laughed. "Elaine, Debra Dunn is a year younger than you are; she's only thirty-six."

"She is?" Elaine looked puzzled. "I read something about her on one of the Internet sites the other day. The piece referred to her as a fifty-six-year-old columnist who is getting more popular by the day."

"Well, I guess that was either a typo or that writer didn't get his information from a reliable source."

"So from which source did you get your information?" she asked.

"Bert Dupont. He also told me that she lives with her father in Parkerton, Indiana. His name is William Overfield and his phone number isn't unpublished."

"Barracuda Bert," she said, using a nickname that displeased the belligerent attorney not in the least. "I see. Well, no doubt Bert has the correct information, but you still won't have to worry about me ever being jealous of a woman who gets off on attacking you so viciously."

"So then you have no objections if I call her tonight."

"None whatsoever. I'd like to talk to her myself and tell her what I think of her malicious news views. But I'm sure that would only get in the way of your secret weapon. Yes, as soon as your palpable charisma comes into play, she'll start writing about what a good guy you are instead of blaming you for the criminal use of Cordell weapons."

"In a perfect world, you might be right. But in the real world, I'll be happy if she will at least be more evenhanded in her reporting." He tightened his arm slightly around her waist and kissed her cheek. "I'll call her as soon as we get home from dinner tonight. I'll be pleasantly surprised if she agrees to a meeting, but there's certainly no harm in trying."

Caitlin stopped herself with one hand on her mother's hip and the other hand on her father's arm. "Daddy, can we eat at Burger King tonight instead of one of those fancy restaurants?"

"If it's okay with your mother, it's fine with me," Ryan answered. Elaine nodded, and Caitlin could almost taste the burger and fries as she skated toward the nearest opening to get her skates off.

After unlocking the door to his apartment, Carl Manning pocketed his keys and stepped aside to allow Debra to enter. She flipped the switch to turn on the living room lights as soon as she passed through the doorway. Having already been here a half-dozen times, she felt almost as comfortable in the one-bedroom apartment as she did in the large house she shared with her father. She tossed her jacket onto a chair and took a seat on the sofa. Carl, who hadn't worn a jacket or sweater, remained standing as he asked if she wanted anything to drink. He sat next to her on the sofa after she declined, saying, "Are you kidding? After the meal I ate tonight I'll be lucky to have room for breakfast."

"Are you telling there's no room in there for *anything*?" he asked as he rubbed her abdomen with a circular motion. His wicked grin, coupled with the southerly direction his hand started to take, prompted her to swat his hand away.

"You'd better be patient for an hour or so before we do anything and let me do some major digestion if you know what's good for you," she told him. Since they had already been intimate on three occasions, he was in no way offended.

"Oh, I know what's good for me all right." He leaned in and kissed her briefly before sliding a few inches away from her. "While you're doing your digesting, there's something I want to talk to you about."

Debra was not at all pleased at how serious his expression had become. The first thing that popped into her mind was that the novelty of dating an older woman had worn off and he was about to give her the "let's still be friends" speech. But then again, why would he do that a few seconds after alluding to the sexual encounter that they both had expected? Could Carl have a cruel streak that so far had gone undetected? If so, he certainly wouldn't be the first man to have fooled her. Case in point was her former husband.

"So you want to talk," she said. "Okay, we'll talk." Although she felt confused, hurt and angry—more at herself than at him for having thought the age-difference had become a non-issue, Debra valiantly kept all of those emotions from showing in her expression.

"You see, Deb, here's the thing. I know we haven't been going out for very long, but it's definitely been long enough for me to realize that I don't want to—"

Debra surprised herself as much as she did Carl by the speed with which she jumped to her feet. "Hold it right there! Spare me the rest of the speech, Carl. I should have known right from the start that you would get tired of being with me and go back to chasing all of those young girls that flit around you at the club all the time. Stupid me, I just didn't think this would come so soon."

"Whoa, girl. I had no idea you had that much of a temper," he said. What got her totally mad was the smile on his face as he got to his feet. He reached out to hold her arm and she batted his hand away. Even as she did so, she wished she'd had the nerve to slap that irritating smile off his face instead.

Debra angrily snatched her jacket off the chair. "May I have your permission to use your phone to call my father for a ride home? I didn't bother bringing my cell phone tonight; I didn't think I'd need it. But don't worry, I'll wait for him outside so you don't have to be around me one extra second."

Now he started to laugh and she gave into her temptation to try to slap his face. He easily caught her wrist and held it. "You are so damn sexy when you're angry. I bet your husband used to make you mad just to get turned on," he said.

"Get your hand off me," she hissed.

"I promise I'll do that, Debra, but not until I finish what I started to say before you went off the deep end."

Although he wasn't hurting her wrist, his grip was so strong that she realized she didn't even come close to having the strength to move until he decided to release her. "Carl, why are you treating me this way?"

Once again his expression turned completely serious. "Deb, I was going to say that, in the short time we've been together, I've come to realize that I don't want to waste any more of my time and effort in dating women I know I could never care for as much as I care about you. I'm sure that, with your type of career, you run into guys all the time who are more sophisticated, more intelligent, and a lot richer than I am, but that's not going to intimidate me and keep me from telling you this: I love you, Debra. And if there's even the slightest chance that you would consider it, I would also love to make our relationship permanent."

Her eyes widened as he said that. "Permanent? Are you saying that you want to marry me?"

"That's exactly what I'm saying, Deb. Wait . . . that's not true, because 'want' doesn't even begin to express how deeply I feel about it. I'd give anything in the world if you would share the rest of your life with me." His soulful look touched her so deeply with its sincerity that tears welled up in her eyes. "I know I'm probably making a complete idiot out of myself because this is much too soon to tell you how I feel, but I just couldn't wait any longer. You are all I think about; I can't help it." None of the extra moisture found its way out of her eyes, but her shock at how much his words differed from what she'd expected to hear prevented her from responding. He released her wrist as if he just remembered he was holding it. Her arm remained raised from a moment, and then slowly lowered to her side while she stood there looking into his eyes without saying a word. "Oh boy," he said. "I don't have to be one of those intelligent guys I was talking about to know what you're thinking. I guess I was a complete fool for even thinking that someone like you would want to be married to someone like me." He lowered his head and seemed to study the floor briefly. When he looked back at her face he said, "I guess I'd better drive you home now. Or, you can call your dad for a ride if you just want to end this here and now."

She thought that he looked as pathetic as a little boy who had just found out his puppy had been hit by a car. "I don't want to call my father," she said. "And I don't want this to end any more than you do." Now tears did begin to slide down her cheeks, and her smile told him they had nothing whatsoever to do with sadness.

It was after 2 a.m. as Debra walked from Carl's car to her front door. The rain had increased slightly and she had insisted that he remain in his vehicle after they'd kissed goodnight. Her father had left the porch light on for her as well as the lights in the living room, but Carl did not drive away until she was safely inside with the door closed and locked. She gave a little surprised yelp as she turned to see her father sitting on the sofa. "Dad, you scared me. You never stay up this late when you have to work the next day. Is something wrong?"

"No. Nothing is wrong. There was a phone call earlier that I wanted to tell you about before you went to bed, Deb."

"A phone call? Dad, you could have just left me a note. You're going to be wiped out at work tomorrow." She smiled. "Maybe you won't be able to outrun one of those nasty dogs on your mail route if you get chased."

He smiled back at her. "There's not a mailman alive who can outrun a dog. How many times have I told you that pepper spray is the only thing that has kept me from getting chewed up all these years?"

"Yeah, yeah, yeah. You're the fastest draw in the post office with that dog spray of yours."

"And don't you forget it," he said. He scrutinized her closely. "You look pretty darn cheerful for someone who has stayed up this late. What's that all about? Oops, never mind. There are some things a father doesn't want to hear about no matter how old his daughter gets to be. Save those lurid details for one of your girlfriends."

"For your information, Daddy dearest, if I look happy it has nothing to do with sex. Carl brought up a subject tonight that totally caught me by surprise."

"Oh? And what might that be? Or is it too personal?"

"It's personal, all right. But I don't mind sharing it with you. Carl told me he loves me and wants to marry me. There, now I bet you're sorry you asked."

"He proposed? Wow, that's really sudden."

"That's what he said. He didn't buy a ring yet, but, Daddy, you should have seen the look on his face."

"What did you tell him?"

"I didn't say yes." She looked at his face, which remained impassive. "But I didn't say no, either. I told him that it *was* really early in our relationship to make that kind of decision, but that I was starting to feel the same way about him."

"Ouch! How did he take that?"

"Not the way you're thinking. We're going to see how we both feel in the near future and, if we decide we should, we'll get engaged."

"And he was content with that?"

"I don't know if that's the proper term, but, yes, he seemed willing to be patient, at least for the time being."

"Did you give him anything at all?"

"What do you mean?"

"Well, when he said he loved you, did you just leave him hanging?"

"I wouldn't phrase it quite like that. I wasn't expecting to hear that from him so soon, or, to be perfectly honest, ever. But I gave it a lot of thought after hearing how he felt, and, yes, before the night was over I told him I felt the same about him."

"Well then, that's settled. I'm going to be the father of the bride all over again."

"Nothing's settled, wise guy. We're just going to see what happens as I've said."

"Uh huh, uh huh. So when am I going to get to meet my future son-in-law?"

"You are impossible," she said. Her smile told him she was enjoying being teased. "The three of us can get together whenever you want."

"Sounds good to me. As you know, my social calendar is totally open," he said. As soon as he saw the look on her face he knew exactly what she was going to say. He was right.

"Dad, maybe it's time for you to start looking for a woman to spend some time with. You're so young and good-looking, it's a shame for you to be alone all the time when you could be dating."

"Ah, Debra, you know I'm not ready to even think about something like that."

"But maybe you should be. Dad, I know how hard it's going to be when you turn fifty-five and Mom is no longer here to make you want to retire and do some traveling as you'd planned. But maybe you should retire anyway and take some trips. You could possibly meet someone on one of them and end up being happy again. It wouldn't hurt to try, you know."

"I'm afraid you're wrong, Deb; it would hurt."

She saw how he began slumping and how his forehead furrowed, and was sorry she'd broached the painful subject. "I'm sorry, Dad. I shouldn't be giving you advice about how to spend your time."

"Honey, I don't mind hearing your opinions, I just don't feel the time is right to even consider replacing your mother with another woman. Oh, sweetie, don't look like that. I'm not condemning you for wanting me to do something about my loneliness. But if I ever do meet someone I can care about, believe me, it could never happen anytime around that birthday that your mom and I had been looking forward to for so long. You understand, don't you?"

"Of course I do." Debra had been standing throughout this conversation and suddenly felt exhausted. She took a seat in a chair across from her father and asked, "I just remembered the reason for you being up so late. Who called?"

"Oh, right. You'll never believe it. Ryan Cordell called about an hour after you went out."

Debra felt goose pimples raising on her arms and neck. "Cordell called me. I'm sorry you had to deal with him. How nasty did it get?"

"Deb, it wasn't like that at all. The guy was as pleasant as could be. And you know something? It wasn't artificial; I can spot that a mile away. We must have talked for more than half an hour. He told me I sounded too young to be your father, and I let him know that I was rapidly closing in on retirement age, but only because I had been smart enough to become a letter carrier. He started joking around about me being chased by dogs as well as their owners looking for the checks that were supposed to be in the mail. And then he got serious and was saying what a tough job it must be to carry the mail. I mean, he sounded like a decent guy I could be comfortable hanging out with."

"Okay, so he won you over, Dad. What did he want from me? Is he talking lawsuit if I don't cease and desist?"

"No, he said he'd like to meet with you and see if you would listen to how he feels about what he does for a living."

"Are you serious? He actually thinks he can convince me that making firearms is some sort of noble profession? I can't believe the man is that naïve."

"All I know is that he asked me to ask you if you would consider coming to Thomasville so that he could show you around his factory and talk with you."

"And of course, that translates into the fact that he intends to pull out all the stops in an effort to have me terminate my crusade to keep public pressure on him and the other companies like his."

"Well, I can't tell you what to do, Deb. That's your decision to make." He got up from the sofa. "I'd better get some sleep."

"Dad, you sound disappointed. Do you really think I should meet with him?"

"Do you want my honest opinion?"

"I always do."

"Okay. I would meet with him if I were you."

"Does that also mean that you feel I've been going overboard with my columns that are critical of his company."

"I don't mean that at all. All I'm saying is that the guy I spoke with on the phone tonight didn't sound at all like some out-of-control demon whose only concern is making money regardless of the consequences."

"I see," she said in a subdued tone. Bill Overfield knew his daughter well enough to perceive that he had hurt her feelings.

"Ah, Debra, don't feel that I'm condemning you for writing the way you have about the subject. I totally agree that something has to be done about the violence in the country. And people like Ryan Cordell are certainly, in their own way, contributing to that violence."

"And yet you would have me drive to his factory in Illinois and witness these weapons being made and listen to his spiel about how 'responsible gun owners' shouldn't be penalized because of the misuse of those weapons by criminals."

Bill sighed. "When you put it that way, you make it sound as if I'm on his side. And I'm not. But maybe, just maybe, you owe it to yourself as well as your readers to listen to what he has to say. Isn't that what journalism is all about? No doubt being open-minded and evenhanded in this particular case is almost impossible. But if any reporter is up to the task, I think you are."

"Wow. That guy really did make a favorable impression on you. Flattery from a woman's father at this time of the morning is not to be ignored. I'll call him tomorrow and make an appointment to meet with him in Thomasville."

He grinned. "Be sure to let me know how it turns out."

She smiled back at him. "You won't be content to read about it in my column?"

"Sometimes I think you are a spoiled little brat," he said. Her smile broadened. "Now I really am going up to bed. I'm exhausted." He took a few steps toward the stairs and then turned back in her direction. "Hey, brat, don't forget about letting me meet your boyfriend as soon as possible. I think I'm as excited about that marriage proposal as you are."

No way that that is possible she thought as he once again headed off to bed.

Kerry Deminski

CHAPTER FIVE

The drive from Parkerton, Indiana, to Thomasville, Illinois, had taken Debra just over an hour. Once in town, she found that Ryan Cordell's directions had been excellent and she pulled into the parking lot of his factory twenty minutes before the scheduled ten a.m. meeting. As she walked inside the front entrance she was a bit surprised that not a single security guard was in sight, and then decided that, with a building full of firearms, guards would be redundant.

"Hi, I have an appointment to see Mr. Cordell at ten, so I'm pretty earlier," Debra said to the factory owner's secretary. "I'm Debra Dunn."

The matronly woman looked up at her and gave her such a welcoming, sweet smile that Debra was positive the woman hadn't a clue as what a thorn in the side of the secretary's boss she was being. This woman obviously didn't read her column and Ryan Cordell, just as obviously, hadn't shared Debra's acerbic writing with his employee. "Oh, Miss Dunn, it's so nice to meet you. We don't often have celebrities stopping in at our little company. I just love your column—read it every day—but of course I don't agree with how you feel about what we do here. As they say, to each his own, though. That piece you wrote about that baby's funeral just broke my heart. I still can't think about it without wanting to start crying all over again." As if to add credibility to her pronouncement, the woman's eyes moistened. Debra, whose career depended on her ability to come up with the right words, temporarily lost her knack of doing so and stood there silently.

After the secretary waited for a moment in expectation for a response, Debra felt she had no option but to give her one. "I appreciate the fact that you like my columns—at least some of them." There. That was the best she could do under the circumstances.

"Oh dear. I didn't mean to offend you. I may not agree with your opinions in the columns that criticize us, but even in all of them, your writing is excellent. I used to fantasize about becoming a reporter when I was a teenager, but of course I never did anything about it. So you can understand how exciting it is for me to meet a woman like you whose work is read in papers all across the country."

This exceedingly friendly and admiring woman had Debra feeling ill at ease. "You didn't offend me." The secretary looked as if she didn't quite believe that. "Really. I'll . . . I'll just have a seat and wait until Mr. Cordell is ready to see me."

"I'm sure he'll want to see you right now. Let me just check." She picked up her phone, spoke to her boss, and then got up to open the door for Debra.

As Debra entered his office, Ryan Cordell was already rounding his desk toward her. He was anything but what she had been expecting. While she had been writing the columns denouncing him and his company, she had always pictured him as old, paunchy and constantly wearing a menacing expression. The ruggedly-handsome man who strode toward her couldn't be more than somewhere in his forties. Also, unexpectedly, he was wearing jeans and a casual shirt with no tie—hardly power attire meant to intimidate her. But dressed down as he was, she noted that he exuded confidence and, perhaps more noteworthy, not the slightest hint of animosity.

Ryan smiled as he held out his hand. "The famous Debra Dunn. At last we meet." She took his hand and shook it briefly. "Knowing in such detail how you feel about the firearms industry in general, and me in particular, I truly appreciate you coming here today."

"I'm certain you won't feel that way after you read my column about this visit, Mr. Cordell."

His smile faded to a grin, but she thought both were genuine and not forced. "Hey, all I asked of you on the phone was the opportunity to present my side of the story. I won't stand here and lie to you and say I won't be disappointed if I'm not able to get my point across. But it won't be the end of the world if I can't convince you that I'm not the demon you believe me to be."

"Fine. I guess we understand each other then, Mr. Cordell."

He cocked his head slightly to the side. "Yes, I suppose we do. But is there any chance we can be on a first-name basis this morning instead of being so stiff and formal? It makes me a little uncomfortable with the Mr. and Ms. business."

"I find it extremely difficult to believe that anything I will say or do during this meeting will have the capacity to make you uncomfortable . . . Ryan."

He startled her to the point of making her flinch when he threw back his head and laughed loudly. He followed that display by saying, "You are some piece of work . . . Debra." She immediately thought that the manner in which he mimicked her with the pause before the use of her first name showed a sense of humor that she would have found endearing if she were dating him. Hard on the heels of that musing came a feeling of guilt; she had been recently proposed to, and he was a married man. Not only that, but he was also a man who had become wealthy making products that caused other people to lose their lives. It was time to move this meeting along to its reason for taking place.

"I will promise you that I'll listen carefully to everything you want to tell me and look at your operation here as objectively as possible. But in light of the way I feel, I can't help but wonder why you even bothered to invite me here." She watched all traces of humor vanish from his demeanor.

"That's the easiest question you could have asked me. Debra, I invited you here to show you firsthand how proud every one of my employees is to be involved with turning out the high-quality products we make. You wrote in one of your columns that I should stop making firearms and look for something to manufacture that couldn't be used for violent purposes. The simple truth is that even if I did that, other companies would increase production and there would be absolutely no reduction

91

in the number of weapons being produced. And, quite possibly, a lot of those firearms would not perform with a degree of reliability equal to those we turn out here."

Debra removed a small notebook from her purse and began to write in it. Without taking her eyes from the paper, she said, "Yes, what a shame it would have been if the Chicago gunman had used a weapon that had jammed instead of a superior, reliable Cordell pistol." When she raised her eyes, she caught the tail end of his grimace.

"Debra, did you know that the police officer who shot Faleski was also using a Cordell semi-automatic pistol? If you knew, you didn't mention that in any of your columns." He wasn't speaking in an antagonistic way, but the accusatory undertone was there.

"No, I wasn't aware of that." Her pen stopped moving. "But what does that prove?"

"It proves that more and more police officers and their unions are asking for Cordell weapons to be purchased for their use. Debra, these brave men and women are putting their lives on the line to safeguard the public every single day, and they know the value of the quality firearms we offer them."

"That would be a convincing argument if they were the only ones being offered your guns, but that is hardly the case. As you know, the Chicago murder weapon was stolen from a private home."

"Yes, a private home where it was legally purchased for protection by the homeowner. How many hands it passed through from that burglar to Ray Falesky isn't really important. What's important is that that particular weapon had been sold by us to a legitimate gun shop and then to a responsible person who lived in a high-crime area and was in need of protection."

"No one, including me, believe it or not, can dispute that occasionally citizens in their own homes use guns to thwart criminals from stealing their possessions or harming them. But if we want to cast the net of truthfulness wider, family members and other innocent victims are killed by accident and during domestic disputes in far greater numbers than intruding criminals," she argued.

"I'll concede that is a valid point. But I, and many other people, feel that the solutions to those unfortunate incidents lie in mental health counseling and better training in the use and storing of firearms."

"I bet it is safe to say that a disproportionately high number of those like-minded people are gun fanatics just like you."

"Just because I inherited this factory from my father shouldn't automatically classify me as a gun fanatic."

Debra gestured at a large display case that contained one of each type of firearm ever manufactured at the company. "I realize those samples of your products are appropriate here in your office, but would it be inaccurate to say that you have an even bigger collection of them in your home?"

"No it would not. And I also have a firing range in my basement for target practice. My son is developing into quite a marksman," he said with obvious pride.

"I see. And how old is your son?"

"Luke is fourteen. Elaine and I also have a six-year-old daughter. Caitlin has dreams of conquering the world of skating just like her mother. If you've watched competitive or professional ice skating in the past, you may remember her— Elaine Snyder."

Debra's head jerked up from her notebook where she had been jotting down his family information. "I absolutely loved to watch her skate. She was one of the most graceful women in the sport. I even went to one of the ice shows in Chicago mainly to watch her skate in person. When she announced she was leaving the sport to get married and have children, I felt guilty for selfishly being sad that I'd never be able to see her skate again."

"You know something, Debra? I felt the very same way. I begged her to continue doing the professional tours even though it would have meant a lot less time together for us. But she wouldn't hear of it." He paused to look out of the window for a moment, and Debra couldn't help wondering if he pictured his

93

wife gracefully gliding over the ice. When he turned back to face her, he was wearing an impish grin. "I've just had a fantastic idea. I've been coaxing Elaine to skate one of her programs for me for a few years now, but she keeps saying she'd be too rusty and she'd rather I remember her as she was at her peak. We have a rink here in town, and I'm betting she could be convinced to do a routine for us after we take a look around the factory. The three of us could go out to lunch afterwards."

"Ryan, how long have you been married?" she asked.

"Fifteen years. Why?"

"Surely after fifteen years of marriage you should realize that your wife is not going to perform in front of a woman who has been so publicly critical of her husband. I'd be willing to bet on that."

"You're on. What do you want to bet?" He clearly enjoyed her shocked expression.

"You can't be serious."

"Oh, but I am. Come on, Miss Debra Dunn, show me how confident you are that you understand women better than I do."

Her eyes narrowed as she studied his expression. "Oh. Okay. I get it now. You're going to try to shame me into pledging not to continue writing about you and your factory if your wife puts on a private performance for us."

"Come on, Debra. Give me a little more credit than that. You're only doing your job the way you see fit, just as I'm doing mine. I was thinking more in terms of the loser paying for lunch today. I asked you to talk with me today only to try to get my point of view across; bribery of any sort is not a part of my agenda. I merely felt that a request from a former devoted fan might be the catalyst Elaine needs to realize that she doesn't have to skate with her former expertise to really enjoy herself on the ice again. I mean, she does devote a lot of her time teaching Caitlin various moves, but I don't think she's ever done a complete routine since she left the spotlight."

"Well . . . buying lunch for three people wouldn't bankrupt me—not that I'll have to because there's no way she'll want to be within sight of me—so I accept the bet."

"Terrific! I'm going to call her right now." He certainly seemed to be genuinely excited about the prospect of seeing his wife back in her element. As he tapped the numbers into his phone, Debra felt as if his suggestion fringed on the surreal, but knew that however the phone call turned out would not affect her one-woman crusade against Ryan and his firearms factory. "Hi, Elaine, you'll never guess what just happened. No, she didn't cancel. She got here early as a matter of fact. Get this: Debra Dunn was one of your biggest fans and asked me if there was any chance at all that you could be coaxed into skating a routine for us after we finish up here. No, I'm not kidding. She's right here. I'll put her on and she'll tell you herself."

Ryan held the phone out toward Debra. Although she gave him her coldest stare, his boyish enthusiasm didn't seem to diminish. "Hello," she said flatly.

"Hello?" Elaine didn't recognize the voice as any of the factory employees, but nevertheless had to ask. "Is this really Debra Dunn, or is my husband trying to pull another one of his practical jokes he thinks are so funny?"

"I'm afraid the only thing he's joking about is that this request was my idea, Mrs. Cordell. When he told me that you are his wife, I indeed did tell him how much I've enjoyed your performances. But under the circumstances that brought me here, I knew there was no way you could be talked into skating in my presence. I even accepted his bet about it because I know I'm right."

After a somewhat lengthy silence, Elaine asked, "What was the bet?"

"That the loser would buy lunch for the three of us. It was nice talking with you, Mrs. Cordell. Here, I'll put your humorous husband back on."

"No, wait."

Debra hadn't moved the phone far enough away from her ear so as to miss her words. "Yes?"

"I *will* skate a program for you and Ryan and then go out to lunch with the two of you."

"You'll do it?" Debra asked in a shocked voice.

"Yes!" Ryan shouted and pumped his fist high above his head.

Elaine clearly heard his enthusiastic shout and said, "Listen to that fool." Her following giggle told Debra that the former skating champion was gratified by her husband's response. "It might be fun to see what, if anything, I can still do."

"Uh . . . I've already told your husband that it's highly unlikely that anything that happens here today is going to change my mind about how I feel about guns and what I intend to keep doing about my feelings."

"Oh, you didn't have tell me that. I can tell from your columns that you're one tough cookie," Elaine said. "I may not agree with everything you write—especially where my husband is concerned—but I do respect your right to your convictions."

"You sound as if you really mean that."

"Don't get me wrong, Debra, I've said more than a few unkind words about you to Ryan after reading your columns criticizing him and his business. But, having said that, I'm not ashamed to tell you that your column about the baby's funeral in Chicago brought me to tears. You are a gifted writer with many years ahead of you during which your news views will have a profound effect on all of your readers. I envy you, due in no small part to the fact that my glory days of skating in public are all behind me."

"I really don't know how to respond to that, Elaine, except to tell you thanks for your kind comments about my writing. Plus, I'm really looking forward to meeting you and seeing you skate again."

Elaine laughed briefly. "You may change your mind if I end up with my butt on the ice for most of my program."

"I don't believe for a moment that will happen," Debra said. "I'll put your husband back on now and I'll see you as soon as we finish here."

"Okay. See you later."

Debra handed the phone back to Ryan. From his side of the conversation she learned that his wife would be waiting at the local rink for them. He was beaming as he hung up. "She sounds almost as excited about this as I am," he said. "You can forget about our little wager; I insist on paying for lunch to thank you for driving this far for our meeting as well as being the catalyst to get Elaine to do something she enjoys."

"Oh no. A bet is a bet, and I'm definitely going to be the one picking up the tab," she told him.

"Since I don't want you calling me a chauvinist in your column, I'll keep my wallet in my pocket at the restaurant. Come on, let's go meet some of the folks who work here."

"You've become one quiet lady," Ryan said as he drove through Thomasville from the factory to the skating rink. "Have you exhausted your conversational quota for the day talking with my employees?"

She watched the well-kept homes and lawns through the windows of his SUV for a moment before speaking. "Your employees all have treated me as kindly as you and your wife have, Ryan. Did you offer them all a bonus to act so pleasant to me?"

"They weren't acting, Debra. They really are a nice bunch of people. I imagine you expected anyone who worked at manufacturing firearms to be evil personified."

"No, I didn't think there would be any horns or tails in sight, but, for God's sake, Ryan, all of my columns about you and your factory are posted on the wall of the break room. So there was no way they should have been inclined to be so nice to me after being reminded of how I feel about your industry every single day."

He chuckled. "My secretary taped them up because she is such a huge fan of yours. She'd asked me if it would be a good idea for her to remove them when I told her you were coming here today."

"And obviously you told her not to."

"Wouldn't that have been hypocritical of me? Now if Rose or anyone else that works for me had hung up a picture of you with blackened teeth and a goatee, I'd have made them take it down. Something like that wouldn't have been acceptable." He flicked his eyes at her for an instant before returning his attention to the road. "Are you starting to regret that you made the trek here to Thomasville to meet me and my workers?"

"Not at all. I know you'd like to hear me say that my kind reception has softened my stance, but I won't lie to you. I'm able to completely separate the goodness of the people from the tragic consequences of the weapons they produce." Debra, who had no necessity to keep her eyes on the road, studied his expression to see if any disappointment would show. It didn't, but still she felt compelled to say, "I'm sorry, Ryan, but I'm afraid I'll never be a supporter of your industry."

"Making a convert of you during our meeting had never even crossed my mind," he said.

She smiled. "Come on now, Ryan. Why else would you have played that video of Rebecca Sinclair gushing over your palpable charisma? Don't tell me that wasn't intended to get me believing what a great guy you are."

"You're as bad as my wife."

"Oh? So she could see right through that little sexpot as easily as I could. Go figure."

"Looks like you're going to get along just fine with Elaine; both of you sound willing to hang me for a crime I didn't even think of committing."

"You expect me to believe that the thought never once crossed your mind during that interview?"

"Aside from the fact that I'm old enough to be Rebecca's father, I am a happily-married man you know."

"Aha! So you're the one."

"The one what?"

"The one happily-married man in the United States," she said.

"Now that's a prime example of cynicism if I've ever heard one."

"Make that a prime example of cold feet," she said. "I've recently been proposed to by a guy I have been seeing for a fairly short time, and I'm still not in the best emotional frame of mind since my marriage broke up."

"Not a very friendly divorce I suppose."

"The divorce was just fine. We had no children, I asked for no financial support, and neither of us had any problems with how our possessions were split. It was just the fact of getting dumped so he could play house with a younger woman that stung."

"Um. I see. So that no doubt is why you immediately zeroed in on those two little words that came off the top of Rebecca Sinclair's head about me when she was wrapping up her little fluff piece."

"I do believe your wife and I would agree that the little tramp fired off those sentiments from a different part of her body," Debra said. She jerked forward enough to feel the restraining seatbelt when he erupted with a loud laugh. Ryan didn't swerve the vehicle even slightly during his outburst, a fact that Debra noted and thought was somehow important, but couldn't figure out why.

"I know I shouldn't tell you this, because you're obviously so paranoid about my reasons for inviting you here, but you seem like a fun person to be around. If things were different, I'd invite you and the guy you're going to marry to go out with Elaine and me sometime. So have you two set a date yet?"

She held up her left hand to display her bare ring finger. "He hasn't given me an engagement ring yet. But he apparently wants us to be married just as soon as possible."

"Oh no! You haven't gotten him pregnant I hope," he said.

She laughed easily at his joke. "We sound like two standup comics trying to impress each other. We'd better be careful around your wife or she'll put me in the same category with your little TV reporter."

Ignoring her comment, he said, "Tell me about him."

"About who?" He glanced sideways to see her looking at him with the question in her eyes.

"About your future husband."

"Oh. Carl is the manager of the only health club in Parkerton. I'd decided to shape up a little and that's where I met him. I was, to be perfectly honest, surprised when he came over and started talking with me."

"How so?"

"Well, I'd only seen him there once before, and on that occasion he appeared to be consumed by attending to the needs of as many young women in the gym as possible."

"By young, I'm assuming you mean even younger than you."

"Oh yeah. Early twenties, if that. But that first time he started talking to me about my column—he already knew about my career, saying he was a fan—all of a sudden our age difference didn't seem to matter to me."

"I get it. You thought he was some old pervert and then you figured out he was only doing his job by dealing with the younger women."

"No, you don't get it. Carl is only twenty-eight—that's eight years younger than I am—and so his attitude toward me took me completely by surprise."

"Hmm. Would I be correct in assuming that he is also in great physical shape?"

"That is an understatement. Not only does he look as if he spends most of his spare time working out, he also is a personal trainer for those people willing to shell out a few extra bucks. Also, he is a licensed massage therapist. He told me he's helped clients get over sports injuries as well as accidents, not to mention the normal aching muscles from strenuous workouts."

"It appears then," Ryan observed, "that after you're married, you'll never have to worry about getting out of condition." Ryan tapped the breaks and then pulled into the parking lot of the skating rink. "Speaking of which, we're about to find out what sort of condition Elaine is in when it comes to doing one of her routines."

As soon as Ryan ushered her into the lobby of the rink, Debra heard the music that added to the enjoyment of the skaters. Ice Dream was set up so that the turnstile, situated between the lobby and the skating area, could be attended by an employee from either the food concession or the skate shop which flanked the entrance. A man was bent over a workbench in the skate shop and didn't look up as they passed through the turnstile. The woman working the food concession waved and smiled at Ryan, and then gave Debra an unmistakably nasty look.

Ryan stopped walking and asked Debra if she wanted anything to eat or drink. "No thanks," she replied and then started walking alongside Ryan. She sensed the food attendant was still looking at her and glanced back. Her suspicion was confirmed, and the look was still unfriendly. "Don't look now," Debra said to Ryan, "but the woman selling the food looks as if she'd love to strangle me."

"I've noticed," he agreed. "She's already informed me that she's written to several of the newspapers that carry your column and asked them to fire you."

"I see. That lunch I've agreed to pay for will take place elsewhere in that case. I don't think I'd have a prayer of eating here without contracting food poisoning."

He chuckled. "Hey, be careful. Remember you said we can't be laughing with each other when my wife sees us."

"Sorry. I forgot. But I don't think she's spotted us yet. Just look at her out there. She looks every bit as confident as she did when she performed."

Elaine Cordell was one of only four skaters on the ice. A man and woman, looking to be in their late sixties, skated arm in arm. A man appearing to be close to Ryan's age skated alone near the outer edge of the rink. Both Ryan and Debra noticed how this middle-aged man seemed incapable of keeping his eyes off Elaine for more than a second or two at a time. She wore a white skating outfit with a diaphanous skirt that would extend midway between her knees and ankles had she been standing still. But this decorative part of her outfit spent its time either behind her or twirling about her hips as she glided and jumped. "Looks like Elaine has a not-so-secret admirer keeping her company out there," Ryan observed.

"Yeah, the guy couldn't be any more obvious if he tried," Debra agreed. "I suppose you can't blame him for looking. Your wife is in fantastic shape. Makes me realize I should be spending a lot more time exercising."

"Skating is great exercise. Why don't you tie on a pair of skates and see if you can steal some of his attention away from Elaine?"

"Oh please. Granny out there is a much better skater than I am. Anyway, all of that staring isn't harming your wife's concentration in the slightest." She elbowed him playfully in his side. "Something tells me you're the one who's getting annoyed."

"Annoyed? Hardly. When you're married to a beautiful woman you have to get used to men staring at her all the time. Actually, it sort of makes a guy feel pretty good. Just ask your future husband how he feels about it the next time he takes you out."

"There you go again. How many times do I have to tell you that flattery is not going to help your cause in any way?" Her smile told him her statement was not to be taken seriously.

"First you make fun of my charisma, and not you shoot down my flattery. You are one tough reporter." He grinned back at her.

"Well now, this is a surprise," Elaine said as she effortlessly skated to a stop a few inches away from them. "I half expected to find the two of you engaged in some kind of bitter debate when you showed up here."

"That's how we spent the entire morning," Ryan said. "We're tired of arguing. I know you ladies have chatted on the phone earlier, but to show my good manners: Debra Dunn, I'd like to formally introduce my wife, Elaine, former Olympic champion as well as the darling of the professional skating world."

"Oh, Ryan, shut up. I'm nervous enough about agreeing to do this." She held out her hand to Debra. "Hi, nice to meet you. I don't mean to be rude, Debra, but I'm going to clear these people off the ice and get started. We'll talk later. Okay?" Before Debra could reply, Elaine ended the handshake and skated away.

"Don't be offended," Ryan said as he witnessed the mildly affronted look on Debra's face, "she always used to get a little standoffish before she performed. Believe me, it has nothing to do with you—she treated me exactly that same way even while we were engaged."

Debra merely nodded her acknowledgement as she watched Elaine skate speedily toward the man who had given her all of the admiring glances. He saw her rapid approach and apparently thought she was going to collide with him as be stopped so abruptly that he grabbed the top of the barrier to stay upright. Elaine skillfully adjusted her trajectory and stopped next to him. Ryan and Debra couldn't hear what she said, but in a few seconds the man left the ice and ended up standing directly across from them. Elaine then chased down the elderly couple— an easy task for her—and they took up a position near a corner at the rear of the rink. The former professional skater then headed toward the front of the rink. As she stopped near the skate shop and spoke to the man working there, Ryan said, "She's telling him to start whatever music she selected for her program."

Elaine glided to the center of the ice and assumed a position with her head bowed and both of her arms raised. A moment later the building was filled with music that was much louder than what had been heard previously. Elaine remained frozen in position, waiting for the appropriate note, and then began to skate. "Oh, it's 'Ave Maria,'" Debra said softly.

The CD reproduced the rich sound of the orchestra as faithfully as if the musicians were right there at the edge of the ice. When the vocalist's emotional words began, Ryan said, "Celine Dione is one of Elaine's favorite singers."

Elaine performed her first jump—a double Salchow—flawlessly, and as she landed, Debra said, "She is definitely one of the best." Ryan wasn't sure if Debra was referring to the singer or the skater, but since the description fit either one, it didn't matter.

The perfect blending of the orchestra's music and the singer's voice was interpreted masterfully by Elaine's movements on and above the ice. Even her facial expressions seemed imbued with religious rapture. Debra looked at the man standing directly across the expanse of ice and said, "Take a peek at the look on your wife's boyfriend's face. She's managed to turn him from horny to holy in less than a minute."

Ryan glanced at the spectator and noted that the man was indeed watching Elaine with no hint of lust. His eyes went back to his wife in time to watch her do a double toe loop and he marveled at how her ability hadn't diminished during her years away from the sport. "Yeah, I'd have to agree that the only thing he's thinking about at the moment is what a graceful skater she is." At the rear of the rink, the elderly couple also appeared to be mesmerized by the skater who had once delighted audiences all around the world.

The number ended with Elaine stopped in the center of the ice precisely where she had been at the start. The difference now was that, instead of being humbly bowed, her head was tilted back as if dedicating her performance to the song's namesake. There was applause given by the sparse audience, and it was initiated by the man standing across from Ryan and Debra. When she joined in, Debra saw that even the woman at the food counter as well as the man from the skate shop were clapping.

Elaine did not bow or wave to acknowledge the applause. She didn't even smile. Instead, she stood completely still with her hands on her hips. The applause faded away, partly because there wasn't a huge crowd to sustain it, but mostly because the people weren't used to a professional skater standing so rigidly after performing. What slightly unnerved Debra, was that the skater's eyes appeared to be fixated on her. Also, Elaine's face, so recently portraying a devoutly religious expression, now seemed to be devoid of any emotion at all.

The opening sounds of the next number caught Debra by surprise and she jumped. Elaine slowly unfastened her flimsy skirt, raised it to her side as far as her right hand could reach, and then allowed it to flutter to the ice. She once again put both hands on her hips and undulated those hips in time to the music. It was now patently clear to Debra that the skater's eyes had been locked on to those of her husband and not hers. When Elaine's hip movements terminated and her skating began, Debra caught the smile that was pure seduction that the woman gave to her husband. Debra felt more like a voyeur than a visiting newspaper columnist as Elaine rocketed across the ice toward the rear of the rink. She couldn't resist the urge to turn her head slightly in Ryan's direction to see his reaction. Debra didn't have to worry about Ryan misinterpreting her curious glance, his eyes were locked on his wife and the woman by his side might as well have been invisible. There could be no mistaking the mixture of desire and love that she saw on his face.

Elaine was skating to Cris Isaak's "Baby Did A Bad Bad Thing" and she shamelessly flaunted her sexuality to the limit as she skated. Ryan knew enough about the sport to realize that her routine would not have passed muster in the professional arena. He had seen so many of her performances and had watched her tapes countless times, so he was well aware that this unrehearsed show was being performed specifically to show him how sexy she still was. Some of the jumps she did were not timed to exactly match the music, and he was positive that two of them had been turned into singles instead of the doubles she had wanted. But nothing she did on the ice took away a shred of the emotion she wanted to impart to him.

Debra was smiling without realizing it as Elaine did a spread eagle and then followed it with a Biellman spin. Her smile grew even wider as Elaine ended her routine with a prolonged shimmy just ten feet in front of her husband. This time she was the first to begin clapping. Elaine skated right into Ryan's arms and delivered an open-mouthed kiss that Debra thought had to contain a tongue enhancement.

"Wow!" Ryan said when the kiss ended. "Had I been a judge I'd give you a ten."

"For the kiss or the program?" Elaine asked.

"Both."

"Liar! You know the second half was far from perfect." She leaned her head in to kiss him again, but briefly and with companionship replacing passion. Elaine, still in her husband's arms, turned to Debra and asked, "Was that worth the price of the lunch you're going to buy for all of us?"

"You were absolutely fantastic," Debra told her. "I'll never forget watching you here today."

"Thanks. I'll get changed and be back in a few minutes." She disengaged herself from Ryan's embrace, skated to the center of the ice to retrieve her skirt, and then made her way to the locker room.

The elderly couple was once again skating around the rink, but the other skater had decided to call it a day. "I think the second part of Elaine's routine was too much for him to handle," Ryan said as he watched the man removing his skates.

"Can you blame him? I bet that was closest thing to an x-rated ice skating performance the guy has ever seen in his life." She managed to look innocent as she said, "I bet there's not a chance in a million that your wife isn't going to give you an even better performance after your kids are sound asleep tonight."

He grinned. "That sounds like something I should be hearing from a drinking buddy instead of a newspaper woman who wants to crucify me."

"Very ironic," she said.

"I was trying to be sarcastic. How was that ironic?"

"Because of your wife having skated to 'Ave Maria' before. Get it? Mother of Jesus? Crucify?"

"Oh."

"And, anyway, that's not what I'm trying to accomplish."

"Then why does it feel like it?" he asked.

Debra looked into his eyes and wondered how he could manage to look so deeply wounded. Was he that good an actor, or did he honestly think he did not have the blood of innocent people on his hands?

Ryan and Debra stood next to her car in the parking lot of the Cordell Firearms Company. She was about to begin the fifty-mile drive home to Parkerton; he was going to walk the fifty or so steps to the entrance of his factory. Debra was anxious to leave so that she could begin writing her column; Ryan was reluctant to see her go because he was certain he had failed to change her beliefs about the weapons industry.

"Thanks again for inviting me here and for being so candid about everything," Debra said as she extended her hand. They were in the process of ending the handshake when she added, "And be certain to thank Elaine again for me for that memorable performance."

"Memorable indeed," he said as he flashed her an easy grin that they both knew alluded to the sexy second half of her program.

"And I was really touched when you went to bring both of your children home from school early to meet me."

"I don't think Luke would have forgiven me had I not given him the opportunity to meet a famous writer, what with his aspirations to write novels in the future. And as for Caitlin, I suppose I just wanted to show you how darn cute she is."

"She is an exceptionally beautiful little girl," Debra said. "But with you and Elaine for parents, how could she be otherwise?"

"Hey now, I'm supposed to be the one flattering you, so cut that out."

She grinned. "Just stating the facts as any good reporter should." Debra opened her car door, but didn't get in. "I'm sure you are a great father to both of them. And from the way that Elaine acts around you, you're no doubt the ideal husband for her." She looked at the interior of her car, but still didn't enter.

"I appreciate the compliments. However, I strongly sense there's a 'but' floating around in your head that you won't allow to escape through your mouth."

Debra put both her hands on the top of her opened door as she stood between it and the driver's seat. She pressed her body against the door, causing it to move a few inches toward Ryan who stood on the other side of it. He knew she was in no way trying to be flirtatious as she looked up into his eyes, yet he felt guilty because he wondered what it would feel like to lean in and kiss her. During his entire marriage, he had never once felt such a strong attraction for another woman, and now, especially after that provocative routine his wife had teased him with, this unbidden urge confused him. He rebuked himself and vowed he would never fall victim to the foolishness of a midlife crisis. "You're right. If it wasn't for that," she motioned toward the firearms factory, "and that," she said as she waved toward the headquarters of the gun enthusiasts he had founded, "I'd have to rate you a ten as an all-around good guy." Not knowing what to make of the fact that he didn't respond, she told him she really had to leave, and then got into her car and did exactly that. As she pulled onto the street, she glanced back to see him entering the factory.

Debra drove toward the first intersection with the events of the morning and afternoon tumbling through her mind and made a snap decision. She hit the brakes hard, made a U-turn, and drove back to the factory. After pulling into the parking lot, she stopped her car near the row of parking spaces nearest the street and backed into one so that she faced the factory and the headquarters of GUN. After plugging her laptop computer into the cigarette lighter port, she flipped it open and a moment later began writing her column.

DEBRA DUNN'S NEWS VIEWS

If I had been told a few days ago that I'd be writing my column in this location, I'd have never believed it. And yet here I am, sitting in my car in the parking lot of the Cordell Firearms Company in Thomasville, Illinois. I was invited here by none other than Ryan Cordell himself. You will recall that I had invited Mr. Cordell to attend the funeral of two victims murdered with a weapon manufactured at this facility. Although Ryan Cordell declined my invitation, there was no way I would have missed this opportunity to observe the millionaire firearms manufacturer on his own turf.

Not only did Mr. Cordell pull his two children—Luke, age fourteen and six-year-old Caitlin—out of school to meet me, his wife, former skating champion Elaine Snyder, skated a special performance in my honor. Elaine's spectacular program was the unequivocal highpoint of my day. While this beloved entertainer hasn't lost an iota of her skill, beauty, and grace, unfortunately, her husband has already lost so many things. Ryan Cordell has lost the respect of every decent person who hates violence. He has lost the right to look any citizen of this country in the eyes without shame because he cannot say, "The weapons that have made me a wealthy man will never be used to injure or kill you or someone you love." Since space is always limited in a newspaper column, additions to this list will be deferred to Ryan Cordell's conscience.

Almost without exception, the employees of Mr. Cordell treated me courteously. Given the fact that my stand on firearms could end up costing some of them their jobs, their lack of animosity was not taken lightly. But as friendly as they were, these Cordell employees did not even come close to matching the graciousness of their boss. I haven't the slightest doubt that Ryan Corell's friendliness toward me was genuine. I just don't think the man could be that good an actor. And that is what made this entire experience so sad. It is always disheartening to be in the company of a good man who does bad things and can't be made to realize it. Perhaps one day Ryan Cordell will look into a mirror and see the image of a man who suddenly knows what the rest of humanity expects of him. If that day ever comes, I would hope that my columns would have played at least a small part in that transformation.

Debra closed her laptop, started the car, and began the drive back to Parkerton. She didn't bother to wipe away her tears; ruined makeup was not at all important as she concentrated on her driving while simultaneously recalling the day's happenings.

CHAPTER SIX

The uninhibited sounds a woman makes during lovemaking never failed to make the union even more exciting for Carl Manning. He increased the pace of his hip thrusts and was rewarded with a faster cadence of moans. Although he could have easily turned the sounds of fulfillment into a duet, he opted to remain silent to better enjoy the sexual song. He waited until the frantic action climaxed before saying, "I wish we could make love like this every single day of our lives."

She smiled. "You know I'd be up for it, but unfortunately my husband doesn't go out of town on business every single day."

He stroked her cheek with the tips of his fingers. "Yeah, Lois, we're going to have to convince him to travel more."

Lois laughed at that, and her movement was pleasurable for him, but not enough to attempt an encore. "Don't expect that to happen any time soon. As for me, I'm just glad I joined the health club and met you. But I still can't believe I'm doing this."

"Technically," he said, "we've finished doing it." He added action to words and gently rolled off her. As soon as he was on his back, she turned on her side to face him. She draped an arm across his chest and nestled her cheek on his shoulder.

After sighing deeply, Lois said, "I wish we could stay here all night. The room *is* paid for until noon tomorrow."

"It is, and it would be great. But you have to be home because your husband will be calling you as usual. And I promised Pete that I'd hang out with him for awhile tonight."

"Pete. Are you sure that's who you'll be hanging out with?" There was no mistaking the petulance in her tone. "I see how chummy you are with all those girls at the club. I'm not blind."

"Hey, Lois, are you forgetting who's the married one in this bed?"

"Don't remind me."

"Come on now. You've told me on more than one occasion how well he treats you," Carl admonished.

"I know. It's just that he's nowhere near as exciting to be with as you are." She moved her hand to touch his well-defined abs. "And he's so flabby it's disgusting."

"He is? Well then, send to the club and I'll get him back into shape. That's what they pay me for you know."

She slapped his abdomen and giggled. "Training him at the same time you're doing me behind his back? I don't think so."

"Why not? Business is business, and pleasure is pleasure."

"Maybe so, but that would be at the top of my list of bad ideas," she said.

"Suit yourself, but don't come crying to me when he reaches the point where he needs a surgeon instead of a personal trainer to get rid of his flab." Carl rolled away from Lois and got out of bed. "I'm going to take a quick shower before I meet Pete."

"I'll join you," she said and scrambled across the bed.

Carl leaned down and put a restraining hand on her shoulder. "No, you won't. I'm already late, and I don't want to start anything we don't have time to finish."

He saw that she was pouting before he turned away, but that was her problem, not his.

Quincy's was fairly crowded as Peter Hatch nursed his second beer of the evening. From his stool at the bar he could see, not only the customers at the tables who were also checking out one another, but also some of the diners through the wide doorway into the restaurant area. He glanced at his watch and then looked at the front door as another patron entered. But it wasn't Carl, so he took another sip of his beer.

Pete Hatch had started working for Carl Manning at the health club several months earlier. After answering a newspaper ad, Carl had offered him the job after talking with him for less than ten minutes. Although Pete hadn't done general maintenance work before, it hadn't seemed to matter in the slightest to Carl. True, the job didn't pay all that well, but Pete had been surprised that his past history of bouncing from one unskilled job to another seemed not to matter to the manager of the club. But what had surprised Pete to a much greater degree was that Carl wanted to spend time off the job with him.

Unlike his boss, Pete was not tall, muscular, nor handsome, and, although he occasionally met women willing to date him, the twenty-three-year-old man's success in the romance department had increased because of Carl. More often than not, when he was in Carl's company and they hit on women, they were successful. He had, in fact, been eyeballing two women who had recently entered the bar and were sitting at a nearby table. There was no way he would approach them on his own, but he couldn't wait for Carl to arrive to see if he would be up for it.

As the bartender walked by on his way to pour another drink, he glanced at Pete's half-empty glass with a practiced eye. Since Pete was a regular, not to mention a fairly decent tipper, the worker wasn't upset about him sitting there taking up space.

"Hey, buddy, sorry I'm late," Carl said as Pete was lifting his glass. "I see you didn't start without me. You got cold feet tonight?"

Pete's lips had been configured to fit the rim of the glass, but they changed to a smile as he turned to Carl and set the beer back on the coaster. Carl often teased him about leaving the first moves up to him when it involved any women they encountered. Since Pete had conferred an almost godlike status to Carl, he never took offense to any kidding. "I was hoping you'd get here before some other guys moved in on those two sitting near the restaurant doorway."

As Carl turned to sit on the stool next to his friend, he expertly checked out the two women without looking at all obvious. "Once again you've proved that you are a connoisseur of beautiful women, but I've come here straight from a horizontal rendezvous. I don't know if I'd have the stamina to do either one of them justice, my man. And you know I have a reputation to worry about." Carl smiled at Pete, and then signaled to the bartender and ordered his beer and another for his friend.

"Were you with your fiancee, or shouldn't I ask?"

"I haven't heard from Debra today. She was supposed to interview that Cordell guy she's been blasting in her column. I don't know when she got back, but I drove out of town right after work to meet a lady who needed some TLC."

Pete grinned like a conspirator. "Aren't you worried about Debra catching you?"

"To tell you the truth, I am a little worried. I don't want anything to mess up my marriage plans."

"I wouldn't either. I know your Debra is too old for me, Carl, but she is one hot-looking woman." After the words were spoken, Pete immediately wondered if his sentiments should have been kept to himself. The last thing he wanted to do was to stop hanging out with Carl and end up back in a dating slump.

Carl looked at Pete with such a serious expression that he wished he could unsay the words. "Pete, I know I can trust you, so I'm going to let you in on something. I've had a lot of ideas, great ideas, about improvements that should be made to the club. When I sat down with the owner and told him a while back, he let me know that he wasn't going to spend a penny on any of my ideas. He didn't come right out and say it, but it was obvious to me that he regards me as some mental lightweight, and that my main usefulness to him is to attract women to the club. When I left his house that night my mind was made up to screw him the best way I could. And that, my friend, is the *only* reason I asked Debra Dunn to marry me."

"I don't get it," Pete said. "That old dude was messing around with Debra?"

"No. As far as I know, he's never even met her. Pete, my plan is to marry Debra, talk her into building me a brand new health club in town, and then taking away most of the customers from his place. That'll teach him that my ideas are worthwhile."

"You mean she makes that kind of money writing for a newspaper?"

"She's syndicated. She writes for a lot of papers. There's no doubt at all that she can afford it. I found a way to check out what she earns."

Pete looked impressed. "What'd you do, use the computer at work to hack into her syndicate's payroll department?"

"I'm no computer nerd, Pete. After Debra signed up at the club, I slept with one of the tellers at the bank where she cashes her checks from the syndicate. That banker lady had no respect whatsoever for Debra's privacy."

"Let me guess," Pete said, "after you pumped her, you dumped her."

Carl laughed. "Can't slide anything by you."

"What about Debra?" Pete asked.

"What about Debra?" Carl echoed.

"Are you going to dump her too after she bankrolls your own health club? Or will you stay married to her and enjoy those big bucks she earns?"

"Come on, Pete. Do you need your eyes examined? Why in the world would a guy who looks like me stay married to a woman who is that much older? Of course I'm going to dump her as soon as I get the club in my name. I've got it all figured out. As soon as finds out she's been had, she'll be glad to get rid of me without worrying about the money she spent for the health club. She is so stupidly sensitive—I've seen her cry a couple of times just talking about some of those sad columns she writes— she'll never fight me in court over money."

Pete looked somber after taking another drink. "Looks like you have got it all figured out," he said.

"What's the look all about? You feeling sorry for Debra?"

"I don't care about Debra," Pete admitted. "I'm going to miss working with you, is all. "You'll be running your fancy new club and I'll still be mopping the floors and putting out the trash at the old place. It's not going to be fun any more after you're gone."

"Is that the kind of friend you think I am? You think I hang out with you only to watch your eyes light up when we get the nod from the women we snag? I was going to wait until the new club was a done deal, but since you seem intent on making me blow the surprise, I'm going to offer you the manager's job there."

"Me manage the place? Are you serious?"

"Why wouldn't I be?" Carl got off the stool. "Let's go see if we can talk those two ladies into celebrating with us. Just remember not to tell them what we're celebrating." Pete followed his friend to the table and, as usual, allowed Carl to do most of the convincing. It didn't take very long to wangle the invitation to sit and talk as a prelude to seeing where the evening would end up.

"I guess he and Pete are making a night of it," Debra said to her father as she hung up the phone. "I should have asked him sooner about going to dinner tomorrow night to celebrate your birthday with us. I'll phone him at work tomorrow."

"Deb, it's no big deal," Bill Overfield said. "You don't have to do anything special for me. I'm sure Carl has better things to do than watch me turn fifty-five."

"Well of course he doesn't, Dad. He is going to be your son-in-law you know."

"How could I forget it when you keep flashing that diamond in my eyes every ten seconds?"

"I do not, and you know it. I think you're making fun of the fact that Carl couldn't afford some humongous stone for my engagement ring. Health club managers don't make the big bucks like you letter carriers."

"Right, I'm not the one pulling down six figures now, am I, Miss Syndication?"

"I know what you're trying to do, but it's too late. I've already bought you a pair of tube socks for your birthday."

Bill chuckled at her teasing, but he was already dreading facing the birthday that had been scheduled to mean his retirement from the postal service and the beginning of a new phase of life with his wife.

Kerry Deminski

CHAPTER SEVEN

The day had gone much better than Bill Overfield had anticipated. Not a single one of his coworkers had mentioned the fact that this was to have been his final day on the job. And since the employees had all eaten a piece of birthday cake during the morning break, they knew without a doubt what day it was. Because he had mentioned his plans so often before his wife had died, he knew they remembered. Being so familiar with the other employees in the small post office, he could just about read their minds as they wished him a happy birthday. He realized his smile was forced and that his good-natured response to the kidding about getting older probably didn't fool anybody. But what else could he do? He had no choice but to get on with his life as best he could.

Now, as he delivered mail on the final block of his route, he let down his guard enough to think about Evie and all the love they had shared before and during their marriage. Despite all the teasing from his coworkers about his age, he felt as healthy and strong as he ever had. If only his wife had been so fortunate, he was positive they could have enjoyed doing so many things together exactly as they'd planned. He looked up from the few remaining letters in his hand at the postal truck waiting at the end of the block. Had this indeed been his last day before retirement, he would have delivered the mail to the last few houses, driven that truck back to the post office, and then embarked on a whole new way of life with his wife. But instead of that, all he had to look forward to tonight was a birthday dinner at some restaurant with Debra and Carl. Not that he didn't appreciate any time he spent with his daughter; she helped him cope with her mother's loss to a much greater degree than he had been able to comfort her when her husband had left. But he felt like just staying home tonight and going to bed early. Maybe then he would have another of his vivid dreams of Evie that he treasured.

Bill stopped in front of the third house from the end of his route. It had been vacant for almost a year, but now a bright yellow and blue sign in the front yard announced that it had been sold. The grass that surrounded the sign was badly in need of mowing, the trees and shrubs in the yard were way overdue for trimming, but it was the house itself that called for the most attention. The aging Victorian had several shutters hanging at different angles, the paint was virtually non-existent, and even the foundation had noticeable cracks and missing chunks. It reminded him of all the work he and Evie had done themselves on the house he now shared with his daughter. The place hadn't been nearly as bad as this one, but bad enough. Looking back on that period of his life, he recalled that he and his wife had done as much laughing, talking, and lovemaking in that empty house as they had done painting, paperhanging and carpentry. Bill stood there looking at the house with his both hands hanging at his sides and could almost hear Evie's musical laughter.

Bill wasn't conscious of his almost-empty mailbag hanging on his shoulder or of the few letters he held in his left hand. Neither did he realize that tears had begun coursing freely down both his cheeks. Only when his chest heaved and a ragged sob tore out of his throat did he become aware of the grief that had overwhelmed him. The distraught letter carrier suddenly felt emotionally naked standing on the sidewalk for anyone to see. Instead of making the last few deliveries and entering his vehicle, he walked onto the overgrown lawn of the vacant house and continued into the yard behind the building. Through his tears, Bill Overfield saw a small wrought-iron table and two matching chairs. He dropped his mailbag onto the ground, quickly sat on one of the uncomfortable chairs, and laid his head on his folded arms on the table.

In this outdoor sanctuary, with only more overgrown shrubs and trees as witnesses, he allowed his anguish to dominate him. The metal table rocked this way and that as he sobbed. He felt as if he would be incapable of living through the day—never mind the rest of his life—without dying of a broken heart. "Oh,

Evie. Evie, I miss you so much," he sobbed. His pain felt every bit as raw as it had when he'd heard her diagnosis, when she had died, when she'd been buried. "Oh God, I can't take any more of this," he moaned.

Ever so slowly, his sobs lessened to the point where he began to think about where he was and that he still had a job to complete. Like it or not, life did have to go on. His only consolation was that neither his daughter nor anyone else had been on hand to witness how poorly he was coping with his loss. Bill raised his head from the table enough to remove his arms and then pulled his handkerchief out of his back pocket. As he was raising the square of cloth to his tear-soaked face he flinched as he saw a woman standing on the other side of the small table.

"I'm sorry I startled you," she said as she regarded him compassionately. "Are you going to be okay? Can I get you a glass of water or anything?"

He looked up into the face of someone he knew was not one of his postal patrons and felt extremely embarrassed. All he could think of to say was, "Who are you?"

"I'm Abby Sterling. I just bought this house a few days ago."

"Oh." He had been holding the handkerchief halfway between the tabletop and his face, and now used it to wipe away his tears. "I'm really sorry about this."

"There's no need to be," she said softly as she watched the cloth move beneath his eyes.

Her short, blond hair was cut in a style that seemed too sophisticated to have originated in one of Parkerton's salons. Even her makeup looked as if it had been professionally done. But she wore faded jeans and a plaid shirt, so he told himself she was no doubt some local woman who took more than an average interest in her hair and makeup. "How . . . how long have you been standing there?"

"Long enough to hear you mention Evie. I'm sorry; I didn't mean to eavesdrop, but I also didn't want to interrupt you. Sometimes crying is the only thing that helps."

He gave her a somewhat sheepish smile as he pocketed his handkerchief. Bill thought he now knew the reason for her stylish hair and makeup. "I bet you're either a psychologist or psychiatrist."

Abby smiled briefly. "Hardly. The only psyche training I had was back in nursing school."

"So you're a nurse," Bill said.

"I don't practice now. I used to be an RN before I married."

"Well, Mrs. Sterling, I wish you and your husband the best of luck here in your new home, but I'm sorry you had to see your new mailman making such a fool of himself." He had a self-deprecating grin on his face as he started to get up, and then sat down heavily as his wobbly legs didn't want to support him. "Whoa! That never happened to me before. Please don't think I'm drunk or anything. I'm not that kind of person."

"Are you sure I can't get you a glass of water? I'm afraid I have nothing else in the house to offer you."

"Thanks, but no. I'll be going back to work in a minute. I still feel a little shaky."

She looked at his complexion and the degree of pupil dilation, which seemed normal for the lighting condition. "Have you ever had any respiratory or cardiovascular problems?"

"No."

Abby walked around the small table and asked, "Do you mind?" at the same time she took his arm to check his pulse. "You'll be fine. You just got a bit upset over your . . . a . . . problem."

It was obvious to him that she wasn't being inquisitive, yet he felt compelled to say, "Evie was my wife; she died of cancer a little over eighteen months ago. Today is my fifty-fifth birthday, and I had planned to retire today so that the two of us could do some traveling and start enjoying life more."

"That's ironic," she said.

"Me having an emotional meltdown today?" he asked with a slightly puzzled expression.

"No. That's completely understandable. My husband died exactly eighteen months before I closed on this house a few days ago. A student pilot crashed into the plane my husband was flying."

"Oh, he had been a pilot. I had jumped to the conclusion you'd married a doctor."

"He was a doctor—a cosmetic surgeon, to be exact—and he had his practice on the coast in Beverly Hills."

"What a perfect location for a plastic surgeon," Bill remarked. "Did he ever operate on any people in the movie industry?"

She smiled. "More than you can imagine. But Tom also traveled to Third World countries doing reconstructive surgery for free on kids and adults who could never have afforded it. He did that through Doctors Without Borders. You've probably heard of the organization." Bill nodded. "He was as much at ease in some god-forsaken jungle as he was at a Hollywood star-studded party. I sometimes traveled with him to put my nursing skills to work, but he insisted that I didn't work with him at his office or the hospitals at home. He used to tease me that he mainly married me because he wanted a trophy wife." Abby smiled brightly, but couldn't pull off the charade and tears started spilling out of her eyes. Unlike him, she had no handkerchief with her, so she wiped the moisture away with her fingers and then dried them on her jeans. "Well, aren't we two of a kind?" She managed to rein in her emotions almost immediately and then sat across the table from him.

"I moved here because it had become unbearable to remain in California around our old friends and acquaintances with Tom no longer there," she explained.

"What made you choose Parkerton?"

"I was born and raised here. I met Tom in Los Angeles in a hospital where I was working." She looked over at the house. "I bought this old place because I wanted to throw myself into a project that would take my mind off what I had with Tom. Now I'm wondering what ever possessed me to tackle something so enormous. I wanted it to be a hands-on thing, and only hire professionals if absolutely necessary. Silly me. I'm afraid I'm way out of my league here. The most I did when I was married was some gardening and a little painting. What was I thinking?"

"It's not that bad once you get started," he said. "When we bought the house I live in now, Evie and I did most of the work. Debra sometimes tells me I should still go ahead and retire and then become a handyman because I'm so good at it. Plus, she says, then I wouldn't have to worry about punching a time clock any longer." He looked at his watch and bounced to his feet. This time his legs cooperated fully. "Good thing I said that. I have to go back to the post office and punch in."

Abby stood as well. "It was nice meeting you," she said and held her hand out. "If you take your friend's advice in the near future and become a handyman, give me a call. I could really use you here. By the way, what's your name?"

He shook her hand briefly. "Bill. Bill Overfield." He looked at the back of the house, which was at least as bad as the front. "You know, if you're serious, I could help you out after work and on my days off. I think it would feel good to put some effort into getting this place back in shape. It is a beautiful house."

"Oh, I'm completely serious, Bill. I can afford to pay you whatever your time is worth, but you'd better be certain your Debra is okay with it first. I don't know if she's your girlfriend or your new wife, but I don't want to cause you any grief if she gets the idea I'm a lonely widow after her man instead of a woman looking for a handyman. I may have been away from small-town life for awhile, but things pretty much never change in places like this."

"Debra? Debra's my daughter. She lives with me. You may even have read her work in the newspaper."

"Debra Overfield? No, not that I recall. Sorry."

"Deb is divorced. She calls her column Debra Dunn's News Views."

"Debra Dunn is your daughter? I *love* her writing. Whether you work on the house or not, I'd really like you to introduce me to her sometime so I can tell her in person."

He smiled. "I know she'd like to hear that as much as you'd like to say it. As a matter of fact, Deb and the guy she's engaged to are going to take me out to celebrate my birthday tonight. Would you like to join us if you have no plans?"

"She wouldn't think I'd be intruding? I've never had any children, but I can see how she might not be too keen on you inviting somebody you've just met, especially on such a sad day for you."

He looked again at his watch and it was obvious he wanted to go, but equally obvious that he wanted to stay. "If you knew Debra, you wouldn't even think that." He took out his pen and pulled an unused receipt from his mailbag. "If you give me your phone number I'll call you with the time and place. Or I can pick you up if that would be okay."

"Of course that would be okay. Give us more time to talk. I'm staying at my mother's apartment in the brick building on the corner of Elm and Second. Here, I'll write down the information for you." He handed her the pen and paper.

"Why don't you bring your mom as well? It is a party after all. Do you have any other family in town."

"Actually, I have nobody in town, or anywhere else. My mom died of an aneurysm the month after I moved back to Parkerton."

"I'm sorry to hear that."

"Thanks." She finished writing and handed the slip of paper to him. "I'll be waiting for your call. I'm going to lock up here now and go back to the apartment to get cleaned up."

Bill tucked the paper carefully into his wallet. He then shouldered his mailbag and said, "If I know Deb, she'll probably want to do this around seven, but I'll call you as soon as I talk to her. So I guess I'll see you then."

"Yes you will," she said and smiled before he turned around and started walking briskly toward the street. "Bill," she called and he turned around. "Thanks for the inviting me to your party."

Although he was far from being in a pleasant frame of mind, Ryan Cordell exchanged brief, pleasant greetings with the people he encountered as he made his way through the building toward the private office of his attorney. Bertram Dupont hadn't been made aware of the visit, but Ryan had no doubts about the lawyer extending him a cordial welcome—that was one of the perks of being the law firm's biggest client.

"What the hell possessed you to pull a lamebrain stunt like that?" Dupont shouted at the instant Ryan opened the door to his outer office.

"But . . . but you told me not to put any calls through to you until you finished going over those briefs." Ryan recognized the voice of Bert Dupont's secretary. The woman was in her late twenties, but her quavering voice made her sound at the moment as if she were in her early teens.

"When the freakin' call is from the governor's office, I take the freakin' call!" The exasperation was evident in every syllable.

The prudent thing to do would have been to come back later in a few minutes. Instead, Ryan closed the outer door and walked to the already open inner door and knocked on it. The lawyer and his secretary were standing almost nose to nose on the visitor's side of the desk. "Sorry to interrupt, Bert." Both of them swiveled their heads in his direction. "Cindy, would you mind coming back in a few minutes to get yelled at some more? I promise I won't break the news to your boss that there is such a thing as a return phone call, so I guarantee he'll still be just as mad at you." Bert looked as if he couldn't believe what he'd just heard; Cindy looked as if she wanted to hug the newcomer for diffusing the situation.

"I'm sorry," Cindy said as she faced her employer again. "I should have known better."

The blustery Dupont, admired within the legal community for always being able to think on his feet, capitalized on Ryan's intrusion. "Aw, Ryan is right. He's the one helping to pay our salaries, not those bureaucrats in Springfield. I'll call them back when I'm good and ready."

That was as close as Cindy was going to get to receiving an apology from her boss and she knew it. As she brushed past Ryan in the doorway, she mouthed a silent "thank you" and received an equally silent wink from him. She gently closed the door after she exited.

"She's a good kid," Bert said in a much quieter tone than the one Ryan had heard from the outer office. "Grab a seat," he said as he retreated to do the same behind his desk. "What's up?"

"Not my morale; that's for sure," Ryan said as he sat in a visitor's chair that was padded almost as thickly as that of his host. "You were right about my invitation to Debra Dunn being a waste of time. Her column about our encounter is just as negative as usual. Have you read it?"

"I have, and I concur. You should have let me fricassee the bitch when I wanted to."

"The funny thing is, except for her misguided views of today's society, she is an extremely likable woman, Bert. But likable or not, her crusade is going to hurt my business and my employees if it continues. I can't keep sitting idly by and allow that to happen. My dad and I have both worked too damn hard to grow the business."

"This is true. So what do you plan to do about it? I hope you have something more drastic in mind than canceling your subscriptions to the newspapers that carry her column." He chuckled as his humor, but hoped to hear that Ryan was now ready to turn him loose in the justice system.

"I came here to instruct you to begin legal proceedings to get her off my case."

"All right!" Bert shouted and jumped to his feet. He charged around the desk and Ryan wondered if a hug was imminent. But the exuberant attorney opened the door and stood in the doorway as he spoke to his secretary. "Cindy, go round up the entire team and herd them into the conference room right now. We are going to take on that know-it-all reporter and get her off of Ryan's back once and for all." He stopped her progress by calling her name as soon as she opened the door to the hallway. "And one more thing, tell the receptionist that nobody takes any calls while we're in there, and that means even if it's from the freakin' President of the United States."

At precisely seven o'clock, Bill Overfield braked to a stop in front of the small apartment building at the corner of Elm Avenue and Second Street. He killed the engine, looked in his side mirror and waited for a truck to drive by and then got out. As he walked around the back of his car, he marveled at all of the conflicting emotions that tumbled around in his mind. The primary one was guilt because he felt as if were about to cheat on his wife's memory. But he was also elated because the beautiful woman he'd met just hours earlier seemed to be more interested in him as a man instead of as a handyman. He felt confused because his daughter appeared to be confused.

A woman came out of the building as he stepped onto the sidewalk, and it took him a few seconds to realize that it was Abby. The plaid shirt and jeans had been replaced by a short, black cocktail dress. "Hi, Bill. Since you told me that the restaurant we were going to is halfway between fancy and schamcy, I thought this might be appropriate. Is it?"

"Oh yeah," he said with feeling. "No one would guess that you had been working at cleaning up an old house all day."

He opened the car door for her. "Wondering what to do first in the house all day would be a better description. You don't look as if you've been delivering mail all day," she said just before he closed the door.

As soon as he pulled away from the curb, Abby asked, "Truthfully now, how did it go with your daughter? Be brutal; I can take it. And don't leave anything out."

He grinned. "I gotta tell you, Abby, I feel totally weird right now. I haven't so much as asked a woman out for a cup of coffee since my wife died. I think Debra was even more shocked than I am about this, if that's possible."

"I see," Abby said. "That doesn't sound very promising." There could be no mistaking the dismal overtones in her voice.

"Shocked was probably the wrong word. Not too long ago she had brought up the subject of me being lonely, and I wasn't ready to even consider attempting to do anything about it. And then when I had my breakdown today behind your house, it just seemed like too much of a coincidence for it to have happened there and then. I don't know. I'm no doubt making much too much of it, but when I saw the sign on your front lawn today showing that the house was finally sold, it brought back memories of when Evie and I fixed up our house. I almost—no I'm not going to tell you about that. Anyway, Debra asked—"

"Hey, I told you not to leave anything out. What were you going to say? You almost what?"

"You'll probably want me to turn the car around and take you home because you'll think I'm a nutcase. I almost thought I could hear Evie laughing when I was standing in front of your house before I made my dash into your yard. And ever since then, I can't get the thought out of my stupid head that Evie was somehow orchestrating our meeting. There. I've said it. Do you want me to drop you back home now that you know what crazy ideas I can get."

"Bill, stop the car." He looked to see if she might be joking with him. "Now!" She wasn't. He pulled to the curb. "Turn off the motor." He complied. "I am having the worst case of goose pimples of my entire life. Here. Feel my arms and the back of my neck." She leaned forward to accommodate his touch. He looked questioningly at her face in the fading light. "I was in one of the front rooms of the house this afternoon and suddenly felt this cold breeze come out of nowhere. All the windows were closed, and I spun around to look at the door, which I had also closed to see now badly it needed varnishing. I thought to myself that the coldness was caused by Tom's spirit arriving to tease me about biting off more than I could chew by buying the house to fix up. And, because it would be exactly something that Tom would do, I started laughing."

"Oh, then I really did hear laughter," Bill said. "At least it means I'm not imagining things."

"No, but as soon as I stopped laughing, I felt incredibly sad. I felt, in fact, as if there wasn't a molecule of breathable air in the entire house. Bill, I hope you won't think that *I'm* the nutcase, but I told you this happened in a front room, so I hurried to the front door to go outside for some fresh air. Bill, I actually was starting to turn the doorknob of the front door when I got this overwhelming urge—almost a command—to go out the back door instead. I did, and saw you crying in the yard. So that's it. Who can say what, if anything, out of the ordinary happened today? Maybe the only important thing is that you and I already trust each other enough to talk about such deep feelings and possibilities." His arm was resting on the console between their seats. She tapped the back of his hand and said, "Come on, let's get to your birthday dinner."

He started the car and pulled away from the curb. "The first thing Debra asked me was how old you are. I told her not to get excited because you were only in your thirties and too young to date her old man. I explained to her that I was going to keep myself busy in my spare time by helping you get your house in shape, and that you were coming tonight mainly because you wanted to meet her."

"Aren't you kind. I'm forty-five."

"You've got to be kidding."

"I wish."

He didn't look convinced, but had yet to meet a woman who claimed to be older than she actually was. "Of course she wanted to know if you were pretty."

"And naturally you told her how beautiful I looked in my work shirt and jeans."

"I did. And then we started talking about which restaurant to go to. Originally, she had planned to go to Quincy's because she loves the seafood there. But it isn't very fancy, and, she said, since I was bringing a guest, we should go to Santini's. So I hope you like Italian food."

"Who doesn't? You should be worried about your daughter liking me instead of me liking the food. I have to tell you I'm more than a little nervous about meeting her."

"You shouldn't be," he said as he tapped his brakes and turned into the parking lot of the restaurant. "That looks like Carl's car over there, so they're probably waiting for us."

As soon as they walked into the waiting area of the restaurant, Debra and Carl got up from their comfortable chairs. "Hope we haven't kept you waiting too long," Bill said.

"We just got here a few minutes ago," Carl said. "I checked on our table though, and it is ready." He extended his hand. "Happy birthday, Bill." Carl glanced at Abby and then faced Bill again. "Debra told me you were bringing a date you just met on your mail route today. Are all of your postal customers so pretty?"

Abby smiled at the compliment, but instantly decided she didn't like Carl. She saw Debra appraising her, and hoped Bill's daughter couldn't tell she'd already pegged her boyfriend as a phony. As Bill made the introductions, Debra appeared to be openly friendly, and Abby was grateful for that. "I don't know if your father told you how much I admire your writing, Debra. I'm afraid my being invited here tonight came about because I told him I'd like to meet you sometime. I truly hope I'm not intruding on your family celebration."

Debra's warm smile erased any doubts Abby had about her sincerity. "Not at all. We think it's great this threesome turned into a foursome." She linked arms with Carl. "Aren't we, honey?"

"Absolutely," he agreed. "But let's make it even greater by getting seated so I can order the veal picatta that this place is noted for." He grinned at Abby. "If you haven't tried it, you should."

"Maybe I will," she said as they started toward the dining area.

After the wine had been selected and their dinners ordered, Abby, who had not chosen the veal picatta, watched Debra remove a small, gift-wrapped present from her purse. "Dad, Carl and I went to the mall the other night to find an appropriate gift for you. This is from the two of us, and we hope you like it." She handed him the present. "Happy birthday, Dad."

"Happy birthday, Bill," Carl said as Debra's father accepted the gift.

"Thank you," Bill said and immediately set to work at unwrapping the box.

As soon as her father opened the lid and removed the watch, Debra said, "I know how meticulous you are about getting your route finished on time and since you told me your old watch was starting to be inaccurate, I thought this would be the perfect present. And don't worry, we made sure it's waterproof, so you won't have to worry about getting caught in the rain."

"You're right, I can put this to good use to keep my supervisor off my back. Thanks, Deb." He smiled across the table at her, and shook hands with Carl, who was seated between them. "I appreciate this, Carl." Bill removed his old watch and carefully stretched the band around the holder in the box before putting on his new watch. He looked inside the box for a long moment before gently closing the lid. "Deb, would you mind putting this in your purse until you get home?"

At the instant when the box touched Debra's hand she remembered that that watch was the last present her mother had given to her father. Bill witnessed the crestfallen look on Debra's face and knew what she was thinking. She kept her head lowered even after she put the box inside her purse that rested on her lap. Bill was not going to let his sensitive daughter berate herself silently for replacing an item that needed to be replaced. He got up, walked around the table and leaned over to give her a hug. "I love you," he said quietly, but he was certain his words were loud enough to be heard by the two other people at the table. He kissed her cheek and then whispered, "It's all right, Deb." Because he stood on the side of his daughter near Abby, she heard the whispered reassurance; Carl did not. Her intuition told her that the old watch had been a present from Bill's wife, although not necessarily the last present.

When Bill slipped back onto his chair, Abby picked up her own purse from the floor. She held its bottom against the edge of the table. "Debra, you might have been wondering why I brought this big clunker of a bag which shouldn't be carried with this dress." Debra's brief smiled showed that the thought had crossed her mind. "I didn't know if you had already given your dad his present or had planned to do it at home after the dinner." She reached inside and removed a gift-wrapped box that was much larger than the one that had held the watch. Abby turned to Bill and handed him the gift. "I want to tell you before you open it that it comes under the heading of a gag gift that is probably a lot funnier to the one who buys it than to the one who gets it. But happy birthday anyway."

Bill Overfield had a quizzical expression that was part grin as he tore the paper to expose a large book. He read the title and then laughed before holding it up so that Debra and Carl could see it. Because of the tentative plans of her father and his new friend, Debra thought that Abby's choice of *What Every Handyman Should Know . . . But Doesn't* was absolutely perfect. What she also thought was perfect was the way that her father leaned over and kissed the cheek of the gift giver. There wasn't a doubt in her mind that, had the two been sitting here alone, the location of that kiss would have been Abby's lips instead of her cheek. Abby uttered the standard response, "You're welcome," to Bill's thanks, but it was the look in her eyes that interested Debra. Her father's love for her mother would always be a part of his life, but Debra knew that his raw pain and his loneliness were over.

133

Kerry Deminski

CHAPTER EIGHT

The dream had summoned a smile to Debra's lips, not only because she was only in kindergarten and hadn't a care in the world, but also because it was Christmas morning. She stood in front of the Christmas tree, with eyes as bright as any ornament on its branches, and shook with delight as she stared at the pink and orchid bicycle that was flanked on both sides with brightly-wrapped presents. "Now aren't you glad you were such a brave little girl and sat on Santa's lap to tell him what you wanted?" her mother asked. Although the bicycle beckoned to Debra, instead of climbing onto its seat and finding out if the training wheels would do their job, she dashed to the sofa to throw her arms around her mother's neck. She was keenly aware of everything connected with the embrace as her mother's arms enfolded her: the way her knees had separated and then pressed against her hips, how her mother kissed her cheek and then her hair, the way that those familiar arms exerted just the right amount of pressure. Debra's happiness was marred by a niggling doubt that something was wrong, but she couldn't figure out what. And then she knew it had something to do with smell; her mother didn't smell the way she should. Debra put her nose right against her mother's neck and sniffed deeply to make sure.

"Mommy, why do you smell like coffee?" Debra was confused, because her father was the only one in the family who drank coffee. She pulled her head away from her mother to look at her father sitting alongside her on the sofa. Bill Overfield stared back at his daughter with the saddest expression she had ever seen. But he remained silent.

"Sweetie, don't you know that I make coffee for your daddy even though I'm dead?"

Debra screamed and sat up in bed. She made the transition from a five-year-old girl to a thirty-six-year old woman in less than a heartbeat. But her terror hadn't ended. She was alone in the house because her father was spending the weekend with Abby, and the aroma of coffee was stronger in her bedroom than it had been in her dream. Her first thought was that some weirdo had broken into her house during the night and was making himself breakfast before he would attack her. It could even be an employee of the Cordell Firearms Company that was going to exact vengeance against her because of her crusade.

Her hand was trembling as she reached for the phone. She yelped when a knock sounded on her bedroom door. "Deb, are you okay in there?" Bill Overfield called to his daughter.

Her muscles went weak with relief as she slumped back on her pillow.

"Honey, I got home really late last night." He hesitated for a moment before adding, "If Carl is with you, I'm really sorry to bother you."

"Dad, I'm alone. I . . . I had sort of a scary dream. Come on in."

He opened the door and stood tentatively in the doorway. Debra sat up and positioned one of her pillows against the headboard to lean against. He looked a bit sheepish, and she assumed it was because he'd suspected she and Carl had taken advantage of his planned absence. "Dad, I guarantee that Carl isn't hiding under the bed. First of all, he probably wouldn't fit because of all those muscles of his. And do you think I'd be wearing these ratty old pajamas if he had come over to spend the night?"

Bill laughed, walked inside the bedroom and sat on the side of her bed. "Just don't start describing any sexy lingerie that you wear for Carl. Fathers never want to hear about that."

"That's a promise I can easily keep," she said. "What happened to your plans to spend your whole weekend off from work with Abby? You two didn't have a fight, I hope."

"No. I do intend to spend the rest of the weekend working on Abby's house with her. But we were doing a lot of talking last night, Deb, and I decided to come home so I could talk to you about it first thing this morning."

"That sounds pretty serious," she said.

Instead of commenting, Bill looked at the three pictures sitting on Debra's dresser. One photograph was of Carl that had been taken at a beach before he'd met Debra. In it he stood next to a lifeguard platform in his swim trunks and it showed his perfectly-toned body that Debra had become so familiar with. Both of the other photos were of Debra and her parents, one a candid shot when she was ten, the other professionally done in a studio when she'd graduated from college. Bill looked away from the photographs to face his daughter again. "Debra, I realize I've known Abby for only a few weeks now, but we've both already reached the point where we feel we belong together. The really ironic thing is that I met her on the very day I had planned to retire from the post office in order to begin spending more time with your mother." He again looked at the pictures, but only for a few seconds. "Deb, the last thing in the world I want to do is have you think I would ever stop caring about your mother, but I truly hope you—"

"Oh, Dad. The last thing in the world *I* want to do is to see you unhappy. Abby has been so good for you. Not to mention how happy you make her." She smiled at him. "So how serious are you two? Are you just going to live together, or do you want to beat Carl and me to the altar?"

"Well, getting married was one of the things we talked about last night," he admitted.

She gave a little squeal and slid from beneath the covers to sit next to him on the side of her bed. "You asked her to marry you? And she said she would?"

He grinned. "It wasn't quite like that. We sort of asked each other, and we both agreed."

"That is fantastic! I am so happy for the two of you." She gave him a hug and a kiss. He looked utterly relieved. "Look at you," she said. "Surely you didn't think I wouldn't be glad about this."

"To tell you the truth, Deb, I was hoping you'd feel this way, but I wasn't sure. I mean, your mom hasn't been gone for very long yet, you know."

She shook her head. "No, not very long, but long enough for you to be so lonely and sad that my heart was breaking for you. I bet that if she can see us right now she's every bit as happy for you as I am." Debra picked up the phone and asked, "What's Abby's number. I want to call her to tell her how good I feel about this."

"Ah . . . Deb, that would make her feel wonderful, but before you call her, I want to tell you more of what we talked about last night." She hung up the phone. "Both of these things were suggested by Abby, but I think they're both excellent ideas. We're going to live in the Victorian and I'm going to deed this house to you. You and Carl can live here if you choose, or buy or build your own house. That's up to you. Abby had said that she recalled you mentioning a few times how much you love this place and thought that would be best. And I have to admit that all of the wonderful memories I shared here with your mother would probably make it a better idea for Abby and me to live in a home that is new to both of us."

"Dad, I do love this house and I know Carl and I will be perfectly content to live here. But I'm not going to let you simply give it to me. You know I'm earning enough from my column to pay you the fair market value of it, and that's what I'll do. You should start thinking about retiring so you wouldn't have to keep contending with all of the bad weather and the hard work. And with your income decreasing, you and Abby could use the money from this house to work on the Victorian and to enjoy your retirement. I know she said her husband left her with enough of an income so that she doesn't have to go back to nursing, but he couldn't have foreseen her buying an old house and fixing it up."

"Well, that's another thing we talked about. Abby told me for the first time last night that her husband's medical practice was so lucrative that he was able to invest an awful lot of money.

She was left with several trust funds and investments that generate an annual income totaling seven figures."

"Seven figures? You mean she makes a million dollars a year? And yet she moved back to Parkerton instead of living it up in Beverly Hills. I mean, how unassuming is that?" She looked at her father and grinned. "I'm surprised you haven't handed in your retirement papers already."

"Deb, Abby told me that her income last year was just over three million dollars. She wants me to stop at the post office this morning and tell them I won't be working there any longer. She wants us to be married in a small ceremony in the Victorian as soon as we get it back into shape."

"What did you tell her?"

"After I joked around about being too old and out of shape to be a boy toy, I told her I'd like nothing more than to resign today. I'm going to do it before I pick her up to work on the house this morning."

"Wow! What a morning this has been. This is all so exciting. Instead of me calling Abby, would you mind if I meet you two at the new house to congratulate her?"

"Better yet," he agreed. "If you want, I can call you as soon as I get there. I can't wait for Abby to see that you have no objections to everything."

Bill was anxious to drive to the post office and turn in his resignation, so Debra walked him to the door to share in his euphoria a little while longer. The phone rang as soon as she closed the door. Thinking it might be Abby calling her father, she dashed into the kitchen to answer it so she catch him before he drove away. She was a little short of breath when she answered the phone.

"Debra, is that you?"

"Yes. Who is this?" The male voice sounded familiar, but she couldn't place it.

"I'm insulted. You don't recognize the guy who signs your paychecks?"

"Sorry, Geoff," she said. "But maybe that's a good thing. It shows that you don't call me very often to complain about my work."

He chuckled. "You have a point there, Debra, but since I'm one of your biggest fans, that's at least one thing you don't have to worry about."

"Oh? From what you just said, and your tone of voice, it appears that there is something I should be worried about. What's going on?"

"I wanted to be the first to call you. I've just learned that a lawsuit has been filed on behalf of Ryan Cordell and the Cordell Firearms Company. It seems that Mr. Cordell is seeking a legal remedy for any present and future setbacks due to the columns you've been writing."

"So Ryan Cordell is suing me. I suppose I shouldn't be surprised, and yet I am."

"To put it more succinctly, Cordell is suing you, the newspapers that carry your column, and my syndicate," Geoffrey Billings advised.

"I see," Debra said. "Serves me right for just now joking about you not calling to complain about my work."

"I'm not calling you now to complain; I just wanted to let you know what I know. Your columns about the connection between violence in the country and the firearms industry have been right on the money."

"Yeah, and now it's going to start costing all of us money in legal fees and settlements," Debra said in a subdued tone.

"Settlements my ass," Billings said. "There's no way that we're going to end up paying Cordell a penny. And, young lady, if you're concerned about personally being responsible for any legal fees, I suggest you reread your contract with my syndicate. It's been awhile since my legal team has had something like this to sink their teeth into and they're already up and running. They just love the smell of legal briefs in the morning." He laughed at his reference to a line from one of his favorite movies.

"I can't believe you," she said. "This could end up costing your company a huge sum of money, and you're laughing about it?"

"You're missing the point, Debra. As soon as the reading public gets wind of this lawsuit, you're going to be helping to sell more papers than ever because of the controversy. I could end up making money instead of losing money because of this."

"I'd have thought you'd be wanting me to ease off on Cordell."

"Hell no! That's the last thing I'd want. You keep doing exactly what you've been doing. Let me and my attorneys handle the legal end of it."

"That's all well and good, Geoff, but I hardly think all of the newspaper publishers will feel the way you do. As soon as they start dropping my column, it won't be long before even small-town weekly papers won't want to hire me after you terminate my contract."

"Come on, Debra. Nobody's getting terminated here. Wait, I take that back. Did you meet Cordell's lawyer, Bertram Dupont, when Ryan Cordell was kissing up to you out there in the boondocks?"

"No, I didn't."

"Well, you didn't miss anything. But, anyway, that little turd will be heading up Cordell's legal team. He tried suing my company a few years ago for wrongful termination of a columnist I'd hired from the Chicago area. Dupont was strutting around in front of that jury with an attitude that the plaintiff thought was going to win him the five million he was seeking. Dupont may have started the trial like a pit bull, but he was a whipped Chihuahua after my lawyers finished with him. I'm surprised that Ryan Cordell is using Dupont. Maybe he didn't do his homework and isn't aware of how we creamed him in court. He'll find out soon enough that Dupont is way out of his league."

"This is all like a game to you," Debra observed.

"It *is* a game. You see, Debra, once you've reached my level in the world of business, simply making higher profits has lost its luster, you need something like this to get the old adrenaline pumping again."

"Glad I could be of help," she said dryly. "But I hope you realize that my reasons for taking on Cordell haven't changed at all."

"Nor should they," he said. "Debra, even though I could never be as eloquent as you on the subject, I abhor violence every bit as much. This new legal wrinkle merely adds a new dimension to the cause."

"I suppose I should—oh, give me a second, I'm getting another call," she informed him.

"That's okay. I'll be in touch again. Tell Hopkins I said hello." He hung up.

Debra took the other call. "Debra, it's Jim Hopkins."

"Jim, this is so weird. I was on the line with your friend, Geoff, when you called and he said to say hello to you. Is he psychic or something?"

Hopkins chuckled. "Or something. He called me a few minutes ago to tell me about the lawsuit. I said I was going to call you to see if you were okay after he told you the news."

"Oh, all right. That makes more sense."

"So are you okay?"

"I guess so. I've never been sued before. I'm not looking forward to it."

"Well, you can't say the same for Geoff."

"So I gathered."

"I haven't seen him so excited since the time he caught a marlin that was twice as big as the one I hooked. Deb, you sound kind of scared about this. Don't be."

"Easy for you to say, Jim. Everything was going so great until this happened. My career, getting engaged, and, listen to this, my dad just told me a few minutes ago that he is going to get married to a woman who bought a house on his mail route."

"Son of a gun! Put him on and let me congratulate him."

"He's not here now, but I'll tell him. Oh, there's more. Dad is on his way to the post office to hand in his retirement papers. His future wife is the widow of a Beverly Hills plastic surgeon and is loaded, Jim. My dad is going to get married to her as soon as he finishes helping her fix up an old Victorian house she bought in town."

"I guess she's not all that loaded if your dad has to work on the house."

"Wrong, Jim. They're doing the work as sort of a hobby. Maybe more of a bonding thing. Dad confided in me that her investments and trusts netted her over three million last year."

"Yikes! Your dad will be able to buy and sell a piker like me."

Debra laughed. "What makes me feel so good, Jim, is the way I've seen him look at her before he knew she was rich. My dad is really in love, and I'm so happy for him."

"And I'm also very happy for you, Deb. How soon will I be flying up to dance at your wedding?"

"We haven't set a date yet."

"Oh? Your guy isn't going to get cold feet, is he?"

"Hardly. Carl, keeps telling me that he can't wait to do it."

"I see. I suppose after what happened with Patrick, you don't want to rush into anything."

"It's not that. I don't know. Maybe it is. Carl couldn't treat me any better than he does. I suppose the age-difference thing is bothering me more than it should. If things were reversed, we might already be married."

"Well, you'll know what to do, Deb. Just don't forget to send me an invitation when you feel the time is right."

"I will, Jim. But for now, I have to worry about this lawsuit."

"You really don't. Let Geoff's people do the worrying. That's what he pays them for. It'll all work out; you'll see. Deb, I'm already late to meet a buddy of mine at the dock for some serious fishing. Promise to call me if you need anything. Okay?"

"I will, Jim. And thanks for your moral support."

"You know I've never had any morals."

She laughed. "Just go fishing and have a good time, you big phony."

There were only a few dozen cars parked in the lot outside the mall, and most of those belonged to the people who had seen the final movie of the night. Dom Penonni couldn't wait to usher his girlfriend into his car and make his getaway. Cheri Morris had to practically run to keep up with her tall boyfriend.

"Dom, slow down. What's your big hurry? You know my mom never gives me any grief when we see a movie on a school night."

"I know your mom is cool. I just don't want to run into those cokeheads again."

"The mall has been closed for more than an hour now," Cheri said. His grip on her arm stayed as tight as ever as she struggled to match his pace. "You know very well those guys would never go to see a romantic movie. They're no doubt hanging out someplace snorting, shooting up, or whatever else they do to get high. You shouldn't let jerks like them bother you."

The big high school jock came to an abrupt halt, and let go of his girlfriend's arm only after roughly turning her to face him. "How do think it made me feel to stand there by the ticket window and listen to them teasing me? You know damn well that if the three of them hadn't known I'll get kicked out of school and have all my football plans messed up, they'd never have been brave enough to hassle me."

"Of course I know that, Dom. But the more important thing is that *you* know it and *they* know it. They know you're going to eventually play in the NFL for a huge salary and that they're never going to amount to anything. You did the right thing by holding your temper. I was so proud of you when you turned your back on them, bought our tickets, and walked inside the theater with me."

He snorted. "Yeah, maybe you were proud, but I felt like the biggest wuss in town. I still do."

"Well, you shouldn't. You did the right thing. I know what'll make you feel better. Let's park over by the river and make out." She took his meaty hand in hers and started walking toward his car, which was parked about twenty feet away from where they had stopped. His car wasn't parked near one of the light poles, but there was light enough to see the three high school seniors that had him upset get out of the car parked on the far side of his vehicle.

"What a coincidence, guys, here comes The Dominator and his hot little piece of ass," Chris Benton said as he strolled around the front of Penonni's car with his buddies at his heels. "Hey, Cheri, if you need to get laid in a hurry, my place is only a couple of blocks from here, you don't have to go all the way to the river. Why don't you dump Captain Chicken and party with the three of us? You know that Bernstein has him on a short leash and he can't do anything about it."

It was Benton's sneer, almost as much as his words, that made Penonni take action. He closed the distance surprisingly fast for someone his size. Chris Benton was lucky that the fist striking his face landed in an area that didn't result in a broken nose or the loss of any teeth. He stumbled back into the arms of his two friends. They didn't have to hold him back from charging toward his assailant—he knew there was nothing waiting in that direction except more pain now that the big football player had lost his temper.

"Stop it!" Cheri shouted and flung herself between Dom and the others as her boyfriend was moving forward to finish the job. "Don't make it any worse than it already is. Don't throw your whole future away over that scumbag."

Chris Benton had been looking at Cheri while she spoke, but then looked at Penonni and, despite his pain, the sneer was back on his face. "She's right, Dominic," Benton said. "As soon as I

145

talk to Bernstein with my two witnesses here, you can say bye-bye to any chance of making the big bucks in the NFL." He shrugged himself out of the grips of his buddies, but wasn't confident enough to take even a small step toward Dom. "But you know, Dom, it doesn't have to be that way. Maybe we can work out a deal so that the school doesn't find out about what you did to me tonight."

"What kind of deal?" Dom asked as Cheri turned from her boyfriend to stand by his side and face Chris.

"Yeah, I thought you'd be interested. Okay. The thing is, I'll be working construction for my old man when I graduate from high school. I mean, I won't be earning as much as you will someday if you make the cut in the big league, but I'll make enough to keep myself happy. But while I'm still in school, I would be a whole lot happier if you contribute enough cash to keep me supplied."

"You mean if I pay you off, you'll keep your mouth shut?" Dom asked. Cheri saw the glimmer of hope in his eyes.

"You got it."

"I think I have about fifty bucks on me," Dom said as he took out his wallet. He was about to crack it open to look inside but stopped when Chris laughed.

"I said I wanted you to make me happy, not insult me. Times that by one hundred and we've got a deal."

"Five thousand dollars? Are you nuts? I don't have that kind of money."

"Well then, it looks like I squeal to Bernstein, and you kiss your career good-bye." Chris started to walk back toward his car. "Let's go, guys."

"Wait! Just wait a minute," Dom said. Chris turned back. Dom turned to Cheri. "My family lives from paycheck to paycheck. I know your mom and dad are split up, but do you think you could talk either of them into loaning me that much money?"

"Both of them claim they're pretty much broke since getting started again after the divorce. I'm sorry, Dom." She looked up into his face as he sniffed once, and then again. Despite his reputation on the gridiron and the numerous fights off the playing field, Dominic Penonni had a sensitive side, and Cheri was not about to let these other three guys see him break down. Her racing mind came up with a plan that just might work. "Dom, I think I know of a way to get the money."

"You do?" he asked. His incredulous expression was mixed with just enough gratitude to make her love him even more.

Witnessing the way the two were looking at each other made Chris feel jealous. "That little plan of yours better work before the week is out. If I don't have the money by Friday afternoon, I'll be spilling my guts to Bernstein. And that's a promise." He went back to his car, his two friends joined him, and he pulled away fast enough to lay two short strips of rubber on the pavement.

As he twisted the dial on his locker, Luke Cordell felt a soft tap on his shoulder. His thoughts about hurrying home to continue reading the latest novel he'd bought evaporated instantly as he looked at Cheri's face. "Luke, will you walk me home? I really need to talk with you."

He turned his head from side to side so quickly that his glasses slid partway down his nose. "Where's your boyfriend?" Luke couldn't help remembering being shoved into a row of lockers on the occasion that had precipitated Penonni's run-in with Jared Bernstein.

"That's what I want to talk to you about," Cheri told him. "I broke up with him."

"You did?" Luke hoped he sounded nowhere near as happy as he felt. He pushed his glasses back into position without being conscious of his action. "What happened?"

"I'd rather talk about it on the way home," she said. "You're not staying late for anything now, are you?"

"No. No, I was just going to put one these books in here and then go home."

"So then will you come home with me? I could really use your help." She was standing so close to him that her breath from that final word entered his nostrils and went directly to that part of his brain where his crush on her still resided.

"You do?"

"I do," she said.

Luke felt that his feet were just about floating over the floor as they walked out of the building. They were still on the sidewalk in front of the school when he began noticing how different everything suddenly seemed. He listened to the chirping of birds in a nearby tree and experienced the very same joy at simply being alive that was so evident in their musical notes. The air he breathed into his body infused him with a degree of energy he'd never, ever been conscious of in the past. Even the warmth of the sun on his face and arms was more like a gentle caress than an annoyance, as he often thought since he was always more comfortable indoors.

Cheri was walking to his left, and he made the conscious decision to shift his books from his left hand to his right to remove that minimal barrier that separated them. As soon as he had done so, she walked even closer beside him, and then closer still. When her bare arm brushed against his, he tingled with excitement although he knew she hadn't purposely titillated him. But no, she continued to brush against him, and had to be cognizant of her actions. He looked down at their touching arms. She turned her head toward him just as he was doing so. Cheri smiled slightly, and then took his hand in hers. When she gave it a little squeeze and continued holding it, Luke Cordell knew, in no uncertain terms, that if he died right then and there, he would have no regrets.

"Luke, remember how I often mention that I want to be an actress someday?" She waited for him to reply and then looked up into his face when he didn't. All Luke could do was nod enthusiastically—he was too choked up to talk. If Cheri was bothered at all by his nonverbal response, she didn't show it. "Well, that was sort of why I broke up with Dom."

"It was?" The tone of his voice showed he thought that was incredible. "But you're so beautiful and smart. Anybody could see you'd make a terrific actress." The words had come tumbling out of his mouth before he'd had the chance to think about them.

Once again, Cheri squeezed his hand. "You really think I'm beautiful?"

Luke knew he was blushing the deepest shade of crimson possible, but had the wisdom to know he had to do more than merely nod. He tried to make himself take on the persona of one of the characters he would someday write about. "I've always thought that, Cheri. I can't believe Dom wouldn't want you to become an actress."

"Oh, it wasn't really that. It was about something I've been asking him to do with me, and he won't."

"Like read lines? Is there a play coming up in school that you want to try out for?"

She threw her back and emitted a throaty laugh. "Something like that. But what I want to do—make that what I *have* to do—could never be performed on any high school auditorium stage."

"What is it?"

They walked along in silence. Because she hadn't answered his question, Luke assumed he probably shouldn't have asked it. But then, why would she have asked him to walk her home to talk if she indeed didn't want to talk?

"Luke, I know you read a lot of novels. What kind do you read?"

"All kinds."

"Have you ever read any novels about women who have rape fantasies?" Luke could not believe what he had just heard, and he again nodded instead of answering. "That's why Dom and I had the fight, and why I told him I didn't want to be his girlfriend any more."

"Oh. Okay. Now I understand. You wanted to rehearse something, but he tried to get you to pretend to be an actress with a rape fantasy to try to take advantage of you."

149

"Good guess. But you have it backwards. You see, Luke, I believe that when I become an actress, I'm going to have to do all kinds of scenes and make each one of them believable. And so I got to thinking about what would be one of the most difficult scenes to do that would have an audience realize the talent of an actress. What I came up with was a rape fantasy in which a girl convinces her boyfriend to play along with her. She would go into her bathroom, take a shower, and come out drying herself to find him unexpectedly in her bedroom. He is already naked, and then she drops her towel. She is screaming and trying to fight him off, but he overpowers her and they do it on her bed. Now here's the part where the difficulty in convincing the audience comes in. After they finish doing it, she tells him she no longer wants to see him because her rape fantasy has been satisfied with him. But she feels driven to meet a new guy to do it all over again. I wanted to do all of that with Dom and videotape it so I could study my technique. He told me it was completely dumb and that I didn't know anything about acting. So I broke up with him."

"It didn't sound dumb to me," Luke said. "Intense, but certainly not dumb. I can just picture how shocked the guy would look when he found out he was just being used and was expendable. And the girl . . . the girl may have been a little surprised herself at how she felt after she completed her fantasy."

"Exactly! I just knew that *you* would understand, being that you're going to be a writer someday." Hearing her say that made that distant someday seem closer than it actually was. "This is my house," she said as she took keys out of her purse and walked up the driveway. She stopped because he was still standing on the front sidewalk. After walking back to him, she said, "Come on. Let's go in."

"I think I should go home now," Luke said. He looked up and down the street, and it was obvious what was on his mind.

"Come on, silly. There's nothing to worry about; Dom and I are history. The only way I'll ever lay eyes on him again is if I go to a football game."

As soon as they entered the house, Cheri said, "Just put your books on the table, I want to show you something." She started up the steps with him following.

She led him directly to her bedroom and closed the door as soon as they were inside. "My mom won't be home for about two hours yet. Take a look at this." She walked to her desk and pointed at a camcorder on its surface. "I had this aimed right at my bed and the bathroom door on the other side of it so that all the action would be perfectly framed. Then my lousy ex-boyfriend had to spoil everything for me." She looked at the camcorder and pouted. "What's the big deal about having sex and taping it?" Cheri made a show of standing with her back to the camcorder and framing the scene between her hands with her thumbs touching. She quickly spun toward Luke. "Hey, will you act the scene with me? Maybe it'll make you want to become an actor as well as a writer. Come on, Luke. Let's do it."

Luke felt as if he had been swept into a parallel universe. "You want me to pretend I want to rape you?"

"No, silly, I don't want you to *pretend*. I'll let you in on a secret, Luke. I didn't even admit this to Dom, but a big part of my reason for wanting to do this is that I've been wondering what it would feel like to be raped ever since I found out about sex. And you know what? Now I'm glad that it worked out this way. Dom and I have had sex so many times, but you and I have never done it, so this is really going to be great. Now you stand out of camera range over by the door until I'm in the bathroom for about a minute. Then you walk over to the bed and start undressing. You can throw your clothes on the bed or on the floor, whatever feels right to you. I'll leave the bathroom door open while I'm taking a shower, but don't walk over and peek inside. Just look at the doorway every now and then as if you can't wait for me to come out. When I do come out, my hair will

151

be all wet and I'll have the towel wrapped around me. That's when you grab me, I drop the towel, and you force me to the bed and we do it. Okay? You ready?"

Luke had begun to perspire heavily. "Cheri, I really like you. But are you sure we should do this?" What he hoped she couldn't figure out was that he wasn't sure he wouldn't mess up. The last thing he wanted to do was to make a fool of himself. That would ruin his chances for having a long-term relationship with Cheri—something he desperately wanted.

They were standing close enough to each other that it took only one step for her to reach him. She wrapped her arms around him before molding her body against him. "I have never been more sure of anything in my entire life," she said huskily. Cheri placed one hand against the back of Luke's head to tilt it forward. His slight intake of breath was accompanied by her tongue, which writhed against his, making him feel simultaneously weak and powerful.

"Now go stand by the door like I told you," she said as soon as she backed away from him. He complied. "And remember, I want this to look and sound totally real. I'll be screaming at you to stop and leave me alone. Don't you dare listen. And I'll still be struggling to get away while we're doing it on the bed, but you use as much force as you have to so that I can't. I'm counting on you, Luke, so don't let me down. You won't, will you?"

He swallowed loud enough for her to hear. "I won't let you down, Cheri. I'll never let you down." He wondered if she comprehended the ramifications of his last sentence. Perhaps, but all she did was to start the camcorder. He was disappointed as she walked around the foot of her bed and then passed by him without a word on her way to the bathroom. But then she turned around and came to him. "Don't worry about this being heard on the tape; I'll edit it out. I know you'll never let me down like Dom did. That's why I chose you to be my new boyfriend. You know what will be totally hot? When you and I make love in the future, we can watch this rape fantasy video whenever we feel like it. I always have a couple of hours after school until my mom gets home from work, so you and I will get a lot of use out of it. So let's make it as good as we can. Okay?" This time she kissed him without using her arms or her tongue, but with their future together now spelled out for him, this kiss left him experiencing a greater degree of fulfillment than the first.

She started toward the bathroom, and then once again walked back out of camera range to him. "You've got me so hot, Luke, that I forgot to tell you not to look at the camcorder. That would ruin the video. Remember, it's just you and me; there is *no* camera." He nodded his understanding. This time she walked slowly into the bathroom without turning back.

Since he was not yet being taped, Luke saw no harm in looking at his watch to time the one minute until he was due to walk to the bed. When half that time elapsed, he heard the water being turned on. Never before had he been so stimulated by the sound of running water.

The second hand of his watch finally crept around the dial and reached the twelve. He took in a deep breath, slowly let it out, and then walked into camera range. His instructions had been to occasionally glance at the doorway to the bathroom. Hearing the shower curtain being opened and then closed, followed by the water splashing on Cheri's naked body, made those instructions unnecessary. But he was careful not to allow his gaze in that direction to last too long. Nervously, he began unbuttoning his shirt. He knew he was still sweating, but thought that was precisely what a soon-to-be rapist would do.

After removing his shirt and tossing it on the floor, he sat on the edge of Cheri's bed and took off his shoes and socks. He stood to undo his belt and fly. She had given him the option of discarding his clothing on the floor or the bed; he chose the floor—that seemed to be more realistic. Now that his pants had joined his shirt on the carpet, he wore only his white briefs. It wasn't embarrassment that caused his hesitation in removing them; he couldn't decide whether to face the camcorder or turn his back on it. In a compromise move, he faced the bathroom

153

doorway with his left side facing the lens as he slid off his briefs. His underwear departed only after snagging on his erection.

It was at that point that Cheri began singing in the shower. The sound of her voice in his aroused state prompted Luke to grasp his swollen organ. It took every bit of his willpower to take his hand away before the inevitable happened.

The water abruptly stopped flowing. Luke heard the shower curtain opening, and knew that he was only seconds away from the time when he must make the transformation from a respectable high school freshman into a lust-driven rapist. He then realized he was still wearing his watch and his glasses. Wouldn't a genuine rapist have discarded both of these items? Although he would have greatly preferred to have a crystal-clear image of Cheri's nude body, he speedily removed his glasses and then his watch. He wasn't sure if he was still in camera range when he walked to her dresser. Both the glasses and the watch were dropped to its surface when Cheri screamed as she came out of the bathroom.

Luke spun toward the shrill noise and almost blew it by apologizing and trying to calm her down. But he managed to stay in character. He advanced toward her with his hands ready to grab. "Luke! What are you doing here? Help! Somebody help me!" she shouted. For an instant, Luke took the time to hope none of the neighbors would hear this, think it was genuine, and call the police. But then she dropped her towel to the floor.

His hands clamped around her upper arms as he began forcing her to the bed. "No! No! How did you get in here?" she yelled.

Luke was surprised by how hard she struggled to remain on her feet, but he was stronger and they toppled onto the bed. "Please stop! Luke, don't do this to me! Oh God! Help me somebody!"

Cheri's head was flopping wildly on the bed, and Luke was being sprayed with droplets of water. Those droplets contained some of the shampoo that hadn't been rinsed away. Its aroma acted as a powerful aphrodisiac on him. Because he was still gripping her upper arms, Cheri's hands were free, and she wrapped both those hands around his throat and began to squeeze tightly. Stunned, Luke immediately released her arms to grab her wrists. His superior strength won out, and he was soon able to breathe freely.

"Help! Help!" she shouted.

Cheri's bedroom door was flung open and Dom Penonni burst into the room. "What the hell are you doing here?" he bellowed as he charged toward the bed. Penonni seized Luke's arms just below the shoulders and roughly pulled him off the struggling girl.

"Oh, Dom, he was trying to rape me," Cheri sobbed.

"What the hell is wrong with you, Luke?" Dom demanded. For emphasis, he lifted Luke completely off the floor and shook him violently. "Why would a little pencil dick like you think you could break in here and attack my girlfriend? I'd beat the crap out of you if I didn't have so much to lose." He set Luke back on the floor. The frightened fourteen-year-old wobbled, but remained standing. "Just get your scrawny ass dressed and get the hell out of here before I change my mind."

All that Luke was capable of doing was to stand there, naked and quaking. He couldn't fathom how the best day of his life had suddenly turned into this nightmare. His eyes were drawn to Cheri as she calmly got up from the bed, retrieved her towel from the floor, and tucked the ends together above her breasts after wrapping it around herself. She then moved to stand directly in front of the camcorder and said, "Cut." Cheri brushed past Luke and Dom, and walked around the bed and shut off the camcorder.

Luke's head swiveled from Cheri to Dom. He was astounded to see that there was no trace of anger left on the huge jock's face. He was even more surprised when Cheri walked to Dom, wrapped one arm around him, and then stood on her toes to plant a kiss on his cheek. "You were fabulous, Dom. Didn't I tell you the little weasel would be dumb enough to believe I

155

could be interested in a geek like him?" She looked smugly at Luke. "So, lover boy, I really had you going there, didn't I?"

"Cheri, why did you do this to me?" Luke asked. Every iota of his anguish could be heard in his voice.

"Put your clothes back on," Dom said, "so I don't have to see that pathetic shriveled-up pecker of yours anymore."

Luke turned his back on them and did as he was ordered. Dom went to the other side of the room, picked up the desk chair, and walked back around the bed to position it between the bathroom and the dresser. "Have a seat, Mister Cordell, and we'll tell you what's going to happen now."

The baffled expression on Luke's face showed he hadn't a clue as to what he was about to hear.

Dom and Cheri sat next to each other on the side of the bed facing Luke. "Here's the thing, Luke," Dom said. "I've got a little problem—what it is isn't important to you—but you're going to solve it for me. You have to give me five thousand dollars by this Friday or else I'm going to—"

"I don't have anywhere near that much money," Luke said.

"Hey, asshole, don't interrupt me when I'm talking. Your old man is the richest guy in town. Five thousand dollars is like nothing to him. You're so talented—what with your plans to be a famous writer someday, you won't have a problem coming up with a story to get the money out of him." He sneered. "Don't all best-selling authors have to have confidence in their ability to come up with believable stories?"

"But you don't know my dad. He's never going to hand over that much money for me to give you."

"He'd better, because if he doesn't, I'm going to give an edited version of this tape to the cops. Do you think your old man would rather fork over five grand or see his only son on trial for attempted rape? And another thing, if you don't come up with the money, I'll also see that Mr. Bernstein gets a copy of the tape. What do you think he'll think of his favorite student when he gets a load of what you tried to do to my little sweetie here?" Dom gave Cheri a one-arm hug. She giggled. "Just in

156

case you have any leftover romantic ideas about Cheri floating around in your stupid head, this was all her idea."

Luke looked at the girl he so recently had thought wanted to be his girlfriend. "Pretty good plot twist, right, Luke?" she asked. "I give you permission to use it in one of your novels someday. That is, if you don't mess up your future by not coming up with the cash. Who would want to read any books written by a guy who had tried to rape an innocent little girl when he was only fourteen?" Her derisive laughter was a sound Luke would never forget.

"Okay, romeo, it's time for you to head home and start figuring out how to convince your old man to part with the money. And don't even *think* about telling him the truth about you being set up. You're smart enough to know what a judge and jury would think if they hear Cheri and me testify and watch the video." Dom watched Luke blink several times and noticed his left leg trembling. He knew the money would be forthcoming and that he'd go on with his football career.

Cheri remained seated on her bed while her boyfriend stood. "Why are you still sitting there? You only have until Friday to get me my money. Go!"

The shouted command resulted in Luke scrambling to his feet so quickly that his chair toppled over. Dom had left the bedroom door open after his dramatic entrance, and Luke wasted no time in dashing out of the room. Even before he started down the steps, he could hear the both of them laughing.

Moving about the kitchen in her graceful and efficient manner, Elaine Cordell displayed no outward signs of her slight depression. Her husband's sore throat had turned into a full-blown cold and he would be staying home from the factory today. What worried her so much more about Ryan, was how depressed he felt over the lawsuit. Although he had never actually come right out and said it, she was certain he felt like a failure because Debra Dunn had gone right on trashing him and

157

his company after her visit to Thomasville. He had confided in his wife that he thought the columnist, except for her misguided convictions, was a likable person.

Elaine sighed as she looked at the empty part of the table where Ryan's place would have been had he not taken another dose of cold medication less than an hour ago. Caitlin was busily eating her breakfast, but Luke's scrambled eggs were sitting there getting colder by the second in front of his empty chair. Elaine hoped he wasn't going to catch Ryan's cold. Last night during dinner, Luke had seemed totally preoccupied and had hardly entered into the conversation. Following that, he disappeared into his room for the rest of the evening.

As soon as she filled her own plate, Elaine said, "I'm going up to see what's keeping your brother. I just hope he isn't getting your father's cold."

Elaine had taken only a single step toward the dining room when Luke walked into the kitchen. He stood just inside the doorway and asked, "Where's Dad?"

"He's sleeping. He came down with a cold last night and just took some more medicine for it." Elaine studied the odd way her son was dressed for school. "Luke, why are you wearing your raincoat? It's not supposed to rain today. And aren't those the pants to your suit?" Since his long raincoat was completely unbuttoned, she also noted he was wearing a black sweater. He was, in fact, completely dressed in black. "Luke, why are you dressed like that?" A niggling concern about her son asserted itself as she noticed the empty, glazed look in his eyes. "Luke, is something wrong?"

"Yeah, Mom, something's wrong," he said in an emotionless voice.

Her impulse was to ask how she could help, but the shock of seeing him slowly remove a Cordell semi-automatic pistol from the pocket of his black raincoat made her lose the ability to speak. All of the target shooting he'd done with his father served him well as he aimed the weapon directly at his mother's heart and squeezed the trigger. Elaine fell backward and hit the back of her head extremely hard on the counter before crumpling to the floor.

"Mommy!" Caitlin shrieked and bounced out of her chair to run to her mother's body.

The six-year-old girl was on her knees with her face just inches above that of her mother as she cried. Both of their faces were wet with Caitlin's tears by the time Luke reached them. Caitlin sat back on her heels and looked up through her tears at her brother. "Why did you shoot Mommy?"

With all of his heart, Luke wished he had the time to explain to his little sister why death was far preferable than living with the shame of what he had been forced to do. But, of course, he had no time.

The second shot he fired that morning also penetrated the heart of a family member. Unlike her mother, Caitlin fell forward instead of backward due to the angle of the round that ended her life.

For a few seconds, Luke looked down at the cross formed by his sister lying across his mother's chest. The religious significance wasn't lost on him, but he had no time to further contemplate it. He kept the pistol in his hand as he left the kitchen and then climbed the stairs.

The door to his parents' bedroom was closed. He turned the knob slowly and then pushed the door open. The thick drapes were closed, but there was more than enough light to see his father's shape beneath the bedspread. Ryan's back was turned toward the door. Luke took one tentative step toward the bed, then another, before stopping. He truly didn't want to see his father's face before he ended his life. It was bad enough that the final images of his mother's and sister's faces were already haunting him.

His hand was shaking, but only slightly, as he aimed the weapon to make another heart shot. He owed his father a swift death, not only because he had always been so good to him, but also because he loved him so dearly.

Luke squeezed the trigger. Ryan bounced once, and then the bed stopped moving.

The teachers at Thomasville High School had assigned, numbered parking spots. The students were allowed to park their vehicles in any of the remaining spots, and, because the lot behind the school was quite large, there was never any shortage of places to park. Dom Penonni drove into the lot much faster than necessary, and then braked hard enough to bark the tires before cutting into a space. "Don't you ever worry about getting yelled at by one of the teachers for doing that?" Cheri Morris asked him.

After he shut off the engine he reached over and patted her thigh. "Nope, that's one of the benefits of being a star football player. I also never have to worry about— Hey, look who's coming. The little punk must have been waiting for us. I bet his old man came across with the money."

Luke angled toward the back of the car on the driver's side, but walked behind the back of the vehicle toward where Cheri sat next to Dom.

"Oh, isn't that sweet," Dom said. "He wants to hand the money to his honey. Roll your window down."

Cheri cranked the window all the way down. Luke bent over to look inside. Dom leaned forward and to his right. "Hey, lover boy, you got a present for me?" Dom asked with a smile.

"Sure do," Luke replied.

There wasn't even time for the smile to leave Dom's face before the round penetrated his forehead. He fell onto his girlfriend's lap and, for good measure, Luke sent another round into the back of the head.

With the weight on her lap and Luke at her door, Cheri could not escape. What she could do was scream, but the other students in the parking lot were more concerned with the shooting than the screaming. They ran off in various directions.

There was no way that Luke was going to shoot Cheri in the head as he'd done to her boyfriend. No, she deserved to know what a broken heart felt like. He placed the barrel of the gun near the center of her chest and shot her.

Cheri slumped forward until her face rested on the back of Dom's head. Luke reached inside the car and raised her torso until her back touched the seat. Her head flopped to the rear over the back of the seat and served to keep her body in a sitting position. Luke marveled at how graceful her long neck looked in that unusual position.

Luke straightened up. A car pulled into the parking lot and drove by, the driver oblivious to what had gone on. The girl parked a few spaces away, got out, and walked slowly toward the school. Luke raised the gun from where he had been holding it down at his side. He kept on raising it until it was aimed at his right temple.

"Luke! No!"

Luke kept the pistol where it was as he looked toward the sound of the voice. Jared Bernstein was running directly toward him.

"Luke! Don't do it!" Bernstein shouted as he rapidly closed the distance between them.

The teacher had no concern whatsoever about his personal safety—Luke could definitely see that in the man's expression. He only wished he had the time to explain to this teacher he respected so much why he had to do everything he'd done. But, as with all of the previous shootings, there was no time.

Luke squeezed the trigger.

Kerry Deminski

CHAPTER NINE

The living room in Abby Sterling's Victorian house was being painted a dusty rose by Abby, Bill Overfield, and Debra Dunn. Abby and Debra were working on one of the walls while Bill painted the ceiling. He was using a roller with a handle long enough to allow him to stand on the floor. His daughter and his fiancee were also using rollers; Abby stood on a stepladder while Debra worked nearer the floor in a stooped position. Bill looked over at his daughter as she said, "I think Carl is going to have to give me a good backrub tonight." She laid her roller in the tray near her feet and straightened up to her full height before raising her hands high above her head.

Bill looked at her, then at Abby, and began to laugh. "It's not funny," Debra said. "Remember, I'm not in near as good shape as you are. I bet if you hadn't been getting so much exercise from carrying mail all those years, your muscles would be aching too."

"I'm not laughing about your aching back, Deb. I just think it's pretty funny that you two are painting the walls and not the ceiling, but you're both totally splattered with paint."

"Yeah, well, maybe that's because we're both in a hurry to get Abby's house finished so that wedding of yours can be held here. Right, Abby?"

Abby smiled down at her from her perch on the ladder. "As much as I am looking forward to that day," she said, "I'm afraid the main reason is that your dad is a much better painter than we are."

"Come on, Abby, you don't have to flatter him; he's not going to chicken out of getting married."

"He'd better not," Abby said. She, too, set her roller in a tray and got down from the ladder. On her way over to Bill she said, "I'm starting to get used to having him around."

"I think what you're getting used to is having a handyman you don't have to pay," he teased. Abby managed to hug him tightly in spite of the long-handled roller he held in both hands. "Hey, stop getting my spotless coveralls all messed up."

"That's what washing machines are for," Abby said. She released him and started back toward the ladder. "Debra, maybe you should call it a day since your back is bothering you. You've been working for hours at this."

"So have you and Dad," Debra said. She reached down and applied more paint to her roller. "And don't forget, I have to stay on the good side of my future stepmother."

Abby laughed. "Are you going to feel weird about that because I'm only nine years older than you are?"

"If I do, I'll just blame Dad for being a cradle robber." She began to move the roller up and down on the wall. "To tell you the truth, Abby, I sort of feel more like I'm getting a sister instead of a stepmother. And I hope that doesn't make *you* feel weird."

Abby began rolling more paint on the wall near the ceiling. "Since I feel exactly the same way, I'll bet this whole thing is going to work out just fine for all of us. Just let's not start calling each other 'sis'—at least not in public."

"You got it . . . sis," Debra said, and they both giggled.

"Jeez," Bill said, "could you two knock it off before my estrogen level increases to the point where I forget that I'm a macho ex-mailman?"

"I think you're just so happy that you're retired now that could care less about which hormones are floating around inside you," Debra said.

"My daughter, the philosopher," Bill said as he grinned and painted.

A warble sounded just outside the door to the hallway. "That's my cell phone," Debra said. "I bet it's Carl calling to talk about what we'll be doing tonight." She removed the phone from her purse, and walked back into the room and sat cross-legged on the floor. It was warbling for the third time before she answered.

"Hello." Abby and Bill kept their eyes on the surfaces they painted. "Oh, no! Oh my God!" Debra said.

Both of the painters quickly put their rollers into the trays and hurried toward Debra. "I hope nothing has happened to Carl," Abby said to Bill.

Bill was more direct. "Deb, what's wrong?"

She held up a hand to request a moment to listen to the caller. "When did it happen? How many?" Her eyes were still on her father's face, but were slightly out of focus. "Are they all dead?" Bill and Abby looked at each other, and he put one arm around her. "I see. Yes, I understand." Debra listened in silence for a long moment. "I agree. Yes, I'll get there as soon as I can. Okay. Uh huh. All right. Good-bye."

Debra broke the connection. Bill could see her eyes focusing again on his face. "Deb, what happened?"

"That was Geoff Billings. He wants me to drive over to Thomasville as soon as possible. Ryan Cordell's fourteen-year-old son went on a killing spree this morning. He killed his mother and his little sister. He shot his father in the back. They think he'll survive, but that he'll be paralyzed from the waist down. Then Luke went to school and murdered two of his classmates—a boy and a girl. It all ended when he killed himself in the parking lot at the high school." Debra set the phone on the floor. "I have to go home to get cleaned up and then drive over there." Having made that announcement, she knew the next step was to get up and leave. But all she could do was to sit there, look into her father's eyes, and wonder if all of the violence would ever end.

It was a few minutes after nine on the morning after the shootings when Debra parked her car in the lot behind the high school in Thomasville. More from force of habit than any concerns about her appearance, she checked her hair and makeup in the rearview mirror before stepping out of her car.

There were some cars in the large parking lot, but not near as many as would have been had this been an ordinary school day. There would not have been three vans from local TV affiliates, each with a satellite dish and several antennas on the roof. The crews from these vans were standing near the rear of the building. As Debra started in their direction, a young woman holding a microphone spotted her. She broke away from the others and hurried toward the newcomer.

Just before the woman reached her, Debra saw that the rest of the herd were now stampeding behind its most vigilant member. With the area near the door now cleared, Debra was able to see a uniformed policeman standing there watching their departure.

"Hello, I'm Rebecca Sinclair. Are you a teacher or a parent?" she asked. She didn't speak into her microphone because her cameraman wasn't in position yet.

"Neither," Debra replied. "I'm a newspaper columnist."

"Hey, that's Debra Dunn," Rebecca's cameraman said as he arrived.

"Better yet," Rebecca said. Debra saw the predatory look on the TV reporter's face as she raised her microphone and looked to ascertain that her cameraman was now recording. "Newspaper columnist Debra Dunn has just arrived at the scene of the shootings here at Thomasville High School. Debra, now that Ryan Cordell will be paralyzed for life and his entire family is dead, not to mention the killing of two innocent students only a few feet from where we're standing, will you finally stop persecuting him in your newspaper column?"

Debra's eyes widened in shock at that callous statement.

The members of the other TV crews jockeyed for position around Debra. One of those reporters was opening his mouth to pose a question, but Rebecca Sinclair beat him to it. "Are you hoping that this tragedy will result in causing Ryan Cordell to become despondent enough to drop his lawsuit against you?"

"You heartless bitch!" Debra spat. Debra tried to sidestep the woman to head toward the school, but Rebecca cut her off.

In the mini scuffle, the microphone banged into Debra's chin. Debra yanked the device right out of Rebecca's hand. "Get the hell out of my way unless you want me to use this as a suppository on you."

For once in her career, Rebecca Sinclair was speechless. The other TV people also said nothing. But they did laugh. Debra slapped the microphone back into Rebecca's hand before striding angrily toward the school.

"She'll find out just like we did that that cop won't let any media people inside," Rebecca said to her colleagues. Once again, she led the pack toward the famous newspaper columnist. She knew Debra Dunn wasn't going to suddenly change her mind and answer any questions; she simply wanted to be as close as possible when the famous woman was turned away by the small-town cop. That minor payback was as much as she could hope for.

"Excuse me," Debra said as she held her press card out toward the police officer. "I phoned the principal yesterday and she gave me permission to come in today to speak with her and the faculty."

"Yes, she told me to expect you," the cop replied. "Her office is all the way down the hall and to the left."

Rebecca Sinclair was fuming as she watched the officer smile at Debra and then step aside to allow her access. She had no more time to waste on spiteful thoughts about Debra Dunn when she spied another car pulling into the lot. Like well-seasoned vultures, the knot of TV personnel descended on their quarry.

Debra spent the better part of the next two hours speaking with the principal, teachers, students and parents. There were grief counselors on hand as well, but they were too busy to approach. She did want to get their insight about the tragedy, but if their duties prevented it, she certainly understood.

From the teachers and the students who'd been willing to talk, Debra learned of the connection between Dominic Penonni and Luke Cordell. One teacher in particular, Jared Bernstein, filled her in on Luke's crush on Dom's girlfriend, Cheri Morris. Debra naturally came to the conclusion that some combination of jealousy on Luke's part, and possible threats against him by Dom over the shoving incident, led to the murders.

During her talk with Bernstein, he told Debra how much he enjoyed reading her work. He also confided that he wanted to become a writer, although fiction was his field and not journalism. That segued into disclosing Luke's aspirations of becoming a novelist. Debra recalled how Jared's eyes had welled up at that point. That show of humanity endeared the teacher to her. He appeared to be about Carl's age—give or take a year—but a totally different type. Jared was a few inches shorter, much thinner, and seemed light years more intense than the man she would be marrying. Debra was walking down the hall back toward the principal's office while having these thoughts. She chided herself about turning into one of those women interested only in younger men.

Stopping at one of the ubiquitous fountains, Debra bent down to get a drink. She let the water splash back out of her mouth until it became a little colder. As soon as she straightened up to continue to the principal's office, she felt a tap on her shoulder and heard, "Excuse me."

"Oh!" she said as she flinched.

"I'm sorry. I didn't mean to startle you."

Debra turned around and looked at Jared Bernstein. If anything, he looked even paler and sadder than he had during their conversation earlier. "Jared, are you okay?" she asked. A heartbeat latter, she said, "That was a dumb thing to say. Of course you're not okay."

"Debra, can I talk to you again? Something happened just awhile ago. I don't know what to do about it."

"What happened?" she asked.

Jared looked both ways to make sure no one was within earshot. "There was a letter for me in my cubbyhole in the office this morning. Debra, it's from Luke." Once again his eyes moistened.

"Oh, Jared," she said as she gripped his arm.

"Will you come to my room so this can be private?"

"Of course."

She followed him down the hall, then around the corner and into his classroom. He walked all the way to the farthest corner of the room and sat at one of the student desks. Only after she took a seat across the aisle from him did he remove an envelope from the inside pocket of his suit coat. He removed the letter from the envelope and handed it to her.

Debra accepted it, but kept her eyes trained on the teacher's agonized face. "Jared, are you sure you should be asking me to read this? I'm really not qualified to help you. Wouldn't it be better to discuss it with one of the grief counselors?"

"Please, Debra."

She bent her head toward the letter.

Dear Mr. Bernstein:

I am dead. Would you believe that it took me more than twenty minutes to come up with those three words to start this letter? I kept writing and deleting, writing and deleting, not being satisfied. But I finally thought: Keep it simple. And so I did.

I chose you to explain why I did what I did, Mr. Bernstein, because I admire and respect you more than any other man I ever met—except for my father. Please understand that I killed my father and my mother and my sister, only because I couldn't stand the thought of the shame and humiliation they would have had to contend with for being the family of a murderer. No matter how many people think I may have hated them, you, at least, will know I loved them.

I killed Dom Penonni and Cheri Morris because they devised a plan to blackmail me for five thousand dollars. Dom told me it was all Cheri's idea. I don't know if that is true, although it may be. I *do* know that I died hating him . . . and loving her.

Mr. Bernstein, I'm writing this only because I feel it is extremely important for society to realize that the cruelty of kids in school will keep on resulting in more and more murders.

Cheri tricked me into pretending to rape her and made a videotape of it. I believed her when she said it was to help with her dream of becoming an actor. After Dom burst into her bedroom, they told me they were going to edit the tape and give it to the police, and maybe to you to humiliate me. If somehow you do receive a copy of that videotape, please, please, please believe me when I tell you I was tricked into doing it. Being a fellow writer, I know you appreciate the irony of a murderer not wanting to be thought of as a rapist.

But the final irony of my life is that, instead of writing novels, I write a letter such as this. Good luck with your writing.

Luke Cordell

Debra looked up through her tears to see that Jared Bernstein was also crying. She reached into her bag for a tissue to minimize the damage to her makeup; he ignored the moisture on his face.

"Now you can understand my dilemma," he said as she handed the letter back to him. "If I simply do nothing, the memories of Cheri and Dom will remain untainted. Society will recall them as two innocent victims of a classmate who snapped and took their lives. If I made copies of this," he held up the letter, "and gave them to the parents of the two students, their memories of the victims will be tainted by the knowledge of how their children victimized Luke. Should I hand this over to the police? The murderer has already killed himself, so what good would that do?" Jared looked beseechingly at Debra while removing his handkerchief from his pocket.

"Jared, did you show me this letter because you want me to ask your permission to print it in my column?"

His expression told her that, at least on a conscious level, that had not been his intent. "Do you think that would be the thing to do?" he asked.

Debra sighed, and then looked out of the classroom windows for a long moment. She began speaking for a few seconds before looking back at the distraught teacher. "I would wager that every other journalist in the country would jump at the chance to be the first to print that." She glanced down at the letter he was still holding. "Not only is it poignant, it is very well written—I would think Luke may well have fulfilled his dream of becoming a successful novelist had things worked out differently. Had I not been campaigning against Luke's father so forcefully in my column, I would indeed ask to print this. But under the circumstances, I can't."

"Yes, of course," he said. "I forgot about the lawsuit that Ryan Cordell filed against you."

"Screw the lawsuit!" she said with a degree of vehemence that surprised her as much as it did him. "That battle will be fought by the attorneys for both sides. I may have been the instigator, but for all practical purposes now, I'm a spectator."

"I see. Then I'm guessing your main concern is how your readers would react should you be the one to print this. You're worried that they would perceive it as gloating because once again your strong beliefs about guns and violence were justified."

"You're partly right, Jared." His quizzical expression showed that he wasn't satisfied with her partial agreement with his reasoning about her motives. But Debra was unwilling to give him any further explanation at the moment. Once again she looked through the windows, and then stood. "I'm sorry that I haven't been the right person to decide what should be done with the letter, Jared. But I think I know who is."

Hospitals always looked and smelled the same to Debra. Those sights and odors inevitably pulled her back to her mother's final days as she walked along the third-floor corridor. The difference between her mother and Ryan Cordell was that her doctors had condemned her to death; his doctors had condemned him to life.

Debra had had no problem in convincing Jared to allow her to show the letter to Ryan. She did have a problem in convincing herself that she should complete this mission. Even if gaining access to him was possible, she hoped she wasn't going to do him more harm than good. That certainly wasn't her intention. And, anyway, how much more can a man be harmed after he has lost his entire family as well as the use of his legs.

By phoning the hospital from the high school, she had learned his room number by pretending that she wanted to send him a card. The woman who had given out that information had added that his condition remained stable. Debra prayed that her visit would not destabilize him in any way. All things considered, she felt she owed him that much.

As she got nearer her destination, Debra paid closer attention to the room numbers. By her reckoning, Ryan Cordell's room was going to be very near to the nurses' station which loomed ahead on her right. She wasn't sure when she reached his room if it had been given him because of his condition or his wealth, but it was directly across from the nurses' station. The woman sitting behind the counter looked up from her paperwork just as Debra was about to turn toward the door to Ryan Cordell's room. "Excuse me, you're not allowed to go in there."

Debra stopped. She heard a conversation emanating from inside the room. One of the two male voices belonged to Ryan, and she was surprised how normal he sounded. She turned toward the counter, took in the adamant expression of the nurse who appeared to be closing in on retirement age. Flashing her friendliest smile, Debra walked over to the counter. "But I hear Ryan talking with someone in there, so I know he's able to have visitors."

"For your information, Mr. Cordell is speaking with his attorney. I've been given specific instructions that they not be disturbed. And everybody knows that Bert Dupont means what he says."

Her smile disappeared upon hearing the name of the attorney that was spearheading the lawsuit against her.

The nurse said, "I couldn't believe it when I heard the news on TV this morning that already the parents of that football player and the mother of the girl are going to sue Mr. Cordell. Those people haven't even buried their children yet and they're planning to see how much money they can get out of this. No wonder old Bert was even more agitated than he usually is. First Mr. Cordell has to sue that know-it-all from the newspapers and now this has to happen to him. Poor man."

"So then Mr. Cordell has been told about everything that's happened," Debra said.

The nurse said, "Yes, he demanded to know, and the doctors allowed him to learn all about the tragedy." She glanced down at her paperwork, evidently anxious to get back to it. When she looked back at Debra's face, it was obvious that the nurse hadn't a clue that she was the know-it-all being sued by Ryan Cordell.

Debra said, "Actually, I'm here with information that Bert Dupont needs about the shootings—information that should be of great help to Mr. Cordell in a lawsuit against him." She leaned over the counter and, in a conspiratorial whisper, said, "No one is supposed to know I'm here."

"Oh dear. You should have told me so immediately. Just go right in. I promise I won't tell a soul."

After smiling her thanks, Debra knocked on the door and then pushed it open without waiting for a reply.

Ryan Cordell was lying on his hospital bed with Bert Dupont leaning in his direction as he stood near the head of it. *"You!"* Bert shouted. "How the hell did you sneak past the nurse?"

"I didn't sneak," Debra replied calmly. "I told her why I was here, and she gave me permission to come in."

"Oh, she did, did she? Well now you have my permission to haul your skinny little ass out of here," he snarled.

"Thanks for the compliment, but go talk to her and you'll see that I'm not lying."

"You're damn right I'll talk to her. And then I'll talk to security and have them escort you out of here." He glared at her as he blustered out of the room.

Debra took advantage of his departure by approaching the bed to stand in the spot he had vacated. "Ryan, I am so very sorry about what's happened. The only reason I'm here is because I've just been given some information that I think should help you."

Except for being much paler than the last time she'd seen him, Ryan didn't appear to be in worse physical shape. His emotional state was another story—a story clearly told by the sorrow on his face and in his eyes. "The only thing that could possibly help me would be for me to suddenly awaken from this nightmare. But that's impossible."

"I know it is, Ryan. And I'm truly sorry," she said. She felt that the way he was looking at her showed that he believed her, but she knew that she was probably mistaken. Debra couldn't make out the nurse's responses to the attorney's reprimands, but a moment later Dupont charged back into the room looking slightly mollified and inquisitive.

"What do you have to show me that could possibly prevent the victims' families from bankrupting Ryan with a civil suit?" he demanded. "Did Billings and his legal team put you up to this?"

"My boss knows nothing about this information," she replied. Now that the moment was at hand, Debra wondered if it might have been smarter to have gone directly to the police or the district attorney instead of to Luke's father. But if she'd chosen the wrong path, she reasoned, it was too late to back away now. Her only hope was that Ryan would not suffer either emotionally or physically from the letter.

"I was asked for help by a teacher at the high school within the last hour. He had received a letter after my first talk with him this morning. Although the letter was sent to the teacher,

Jared Bernstein, it is of infinitely more value to you, Ryan." She took the envelope from her purse, removed the letter, and held it out to the patient. "The letter is from Luke."

Ryan gasped at the mention of his son's name. His hand trembled as he accepted the piece of paper.

Debra glanced at the attorney, whose eyes were riveted on his client, and then she walked away from the bed to stand next to the window. She kept her back to the outside world, however, and keenly observed Ryan Cordell's face as he read. Both she and Dupont saw the tears spill out of Ryan's eyes and begin coursing down his cheeks. Her reaction was to fold her arms across her chest and hunch her shoulders. The attorney coughed nervously, and then looked at Debra with a slightly belligerent expression as if to ward off any suspicions on her part that he was less than macho.

Ryan finished reading, and then lay the letter face down on his chest while still gripping it. A moment later he handed it to Bert. He took the letter and then walked toward Debra. "Let me get some better light."

She walked away from the window and he took her place. After placing the letter on the wide windowsill, he bent his head and began to read while keeping his back to the others.

"Those bastards!" Debra and Ryan both knew which part of the letter he had reached.

The attorney finished reading and raised his head. He then removed his handkerchief and blew his nose noisily. His back was still toward the patient and the columnist, but they could tell that he was wiping both his eyes with the handkerchief. He returned it to his pocket, coughed again, and then picked up the letter before returning to the others.

"Ryan, I have to use this to have a judge issue a search warrant so the police can locate that videotape and any copies before either family finds and destroys them. I'm sure those people don't know about this, but we can't take any chances." He tapped the letter. "This by itself would greatly increase your chances of winning the decision, but there's no way they can get

175

a penny out of you if the police locate that tape. That's the smoking gun we need." As soon as those last words left his mouth, Bert Dupont looked stricken. "Aw, Jesus, Ryan. That was incredibly stupid of me. I'm sorry."

"It's okay, Bert," Ryan said softly.

The attorney's look showed that it wasn't okay, but he had no time to waste on dwelling on his thoughtless comment. "I have to leave right now and get moving on this," he announced. He reached over and touched Ryan's shoulder. "Hang in there. I'll be back later to check up on you and fill you in on this."

Bert Dupont walked past Debra without even glancing at her on his way to the door. When he got there, he stood with his hand on the doorknob without turning it. Then he sighed, turned around and walked over to stand in front of her. "I'm not very good at this sort of thing. I get paid to tear apart my adversaries any which way I can. And anybody who knows me will tell you that I totally get off on a good courtroom battle. Believe me when I tell you that I was going to fight tooth and nail to get a judgement against you and the other defendants in the lawsuit. But after what you've just done for my client, my heart just wouldn't be in it." He looked at the patient. "Ryan, I'm sorry, but you're going to have to find another law firm to go up against the newspapers. And if you no longer want me to represent your company in other matters, I'll understand. But let me take care of this for you," he slapped the letter against his other hand, "so I can be certain there aren't any slipups." Without waiting for a response, Bert Dupont turned around and left the room.

The vacuum left by the energetic attorney's departure drew Debra closer to the hospital bed. "Is he always so hyper?" she asked.

"Hard to believe, but Bert isn't usually so subdued. All of this has him hovering around me like a guardian angel."

"That's understandable. You're not going to stop using his services, are you? He'll probably come to his senses shortly and regain his appetite for building your case against me and the other defendants. I'm certain any other person in my shoes would have brought that letter to you."

"Don't bet on that. It took a lot of integrity to do what you did, not to mention compassion. I can't help but wonder how many people in your position would have published that letter instead of bringing it to me. I'll never forget this, Debra. And as far as Bert is concerned, I—oh!"

"I'll go get the nurse," Debra said as Ryan's face contorted with pain.

"No. Don't." She had made it halfway to the door, but returned to the bed. "I'm okay. Just a jolt of pain I hadn't expected." He gestured toward the IV stand on the opposite side of the bed from where she stood. "I can take more of that painkiller anytime I want to by pressing that button."

"Well then, Ryan, for goodness sake, press the button."

"I will if it gets too bad. But it makes me groggy and I can't think straight."

She looked at the medication and then back at his face, which once again had returned to as normal as could be expected. "If ever there was a time in your life when you'd be better off not thinking straight, this is it. I think I'm going to go so that you won't feel obligated to carry on a conversation."

"A conversation is about all I will be able to carry from now on," he said as looked down at the lower half of his body. "Oh boy, listen to me. I spend every second that I'm not thinking about my family pledging to myself that I won't wallow in self-pity because my walking days are over. And I couldn't even make it through the first few hours after I found out." She couldn't think of a single thing that would be appropriate to say to him. That inability was clearly displayed on her face. "Debra, you can leave. It's okay. I'm sure that there are a lot of people in town you want to interview for your column. That's your job. That's why you came to Thomasville; I understand."

"Do you want me to stay?"

"Do you want to stay?"

She turned around and walked toward the door, but passed it and began dragging a heavy chair from the corner of the room back to the bed. As soon as she was seated, she said, "Since I brought the letter, I'll stay until Bert comes back to find out if the videotape was found. Is that okay?"

"Why wouldn't it be?" he asked.

"In spite of the possibility that my bringing the letter may help with one of your problems, I can hardly be described as a person you'd want to spend any time with."

"Not true. Elaine and I totally enjoyed your last visit to Thomasville." Unbidden, tears filled his eyes, spilled out, and then ran down his cheeks. He grimaced as he extended an arm toward the box of tissues on the stand near his bed. She was instantly on her feet. After handing him several of the tissues, she placed the box on the bed next to him. He began wiping his face while she sat back down. "Maybe you'd be better off waiting for Bert down the hall in the solarium. I can't think of my wife or kids without breaking down. I don't want to put you through watching me doing this. All of this is my fault; not yours."

"Ryan! What a terrible thing to say. This isn't your fault. *None* of this is your fault. How can you even think such a thing?"

"Debra, my son got the pistol from the shooting range I had constructed in the basement of our house. Elaine had always been terrified of guns and had never once even set foot in that room. Caitlin, I felt, was too young to be allowed in there when Luke and I practiced, and, of course, I never let her so much as touch a weapon. But she was such a curious little girl, I was afraid she might somehow get the opportunity to unlock that door if I kept the key on my key ring. I thought I was been so clever when I hid the key on top of the molding over the door to the room with the weapons. She didn't even know it was there. Luke, on the other hand, did." He was crying again, and Debra made no attempt to get him to stop. Crying and talking, she was certain, were the two activities that he should be engaged in. His emotional recovery would be a long and difficult process, but he had already begun it, and Debra felt somehow grateful to be a small part of it.

"Luke had always been kind of a quiet kid who liked to spend a lot of time alone. Maybe kids that eventually want to become writers are like that; I don't know. But now, after what happened, I keep asking myself if I could have missed some sign—some telling signal—that Luke needed psychological help that would have prevented it from happening. If only I'd had the wisdom to see that he needed help, nobody would have died and Luke could have gone on to try to become the author he knew he could be. But of course I wasn't that wise. I wasn't even smart enough to realize that he shouldn't have been shown where I kept the key to the shooting range."

"I'm sure this guilt you're feeling is normal, no matter how irrational it may be. Ryan, I've written more than one column about the benefits of grief counseling with a professional, as well as joining groups whose members are experiencing the same emotions. I'm convinced they do a lot of good for a lot of people. I hope you consider looking into that as soon as you can."

"You know what? I will." He looked at her with what she assumed was gratitude. But his features scrunched up into what she was positive signified pain—physical pain. He managed not to make any sound, and hung on until it subsided slightly before saying, "I'm afraid I'm going to need some more medication." He took a deep breath, and then let it out with deliberate slowness. "Debra, before I get all doped up here, I was starting to tell you something before, and then it slipped my mind. I'm going to instruct Bert to cancel the proceedings against you, your syndicate, and the newspapers. What a horrible price my family as well as those two kids had to pay before I realized the truth. You were right; I was wrong. If only I had realized that sooner, I would have—oh, dear God, this hurts."

Ryan's hand was trembling as he reached for the button that would immediately send the colorless liquid coursing through his

179

circulatory system. Debra watched his finger press the button once, and then a second time. She was fairly certain that the tears running down his face now were brought on by the physical pain from the wound rather than the heartache he was dealing with.

Lunchtime had come and gone with neither Debra nor Ryan having eaten. His lunch sat on the wheeled tray table; what could have been hers remained in the hospital cafeteria. Ryan had been sleeping ever since the painkiller had kicked in, and Debra had agreed with the orderly who had delivered his food that this particular patient had more need of temporary forgetfulness than sustenance. Debra wasn't quite sure why she felt it more important to sit quietly next to the bed instead of heading down to the cafeteria on the first floor. Probably, she told herself, she maintained her vigil so as not to miss a single word of Bert Dupont's disclosure. Perhaps, but Debra felt an overwhelming degree of pity for Ryan Cordell, and hoped that her presence would be of some benefit to him, no matter how small.

Debra hadn't heard any footsteps and Bert didn't knock before entering. "Ryan, I'm back," he announced before ascertaining that his client was sleeping.

"Sh. Please don't wake him up," Debra said.

"What are you still doing here?" he demanded in a gruff voice. Debra managed not to smile as she watched his expression soften. She was positive he'd used that brief period of time to remember that he was no longer going to face off against her in court because of her handing over the letter from Luke. "Sorry. Has he been sleeping long?"

"Quite awhile. His lunch is still sitting there," she said and then gestured at the table. "He was in a lot of pain, and the medication he took did it for him."

The attorney looked at Ryan's face, from which even the powerful medication couldn't remove the sorrow. "As good as my news is, it'll keep until he wakes up on his own. Any extra second he spends unconscious has to be precious to him." He turned toward Debra. "Since you're the one who brought the information here to us, do you want to hear what's happened with it? I'm sure you've had your lunch, but I haven't had time to eat and I'm starving. You want to come down to the cafeteria and have a cup of coffee or something?"

"Actually, I haven't eaten either. Let's go."

Their walk and elevator ride was accomplished with a minimum of conversation. And while selecting and paying for their meals they spoke only with the cafeteria employees. Bert had eaten most of his first slice of pizza before Debra, unable to wait any longer, asked, "So was the letter enough to convince a judge to issue a search warrant?"

"Oh yeah," the attorney replied. "She agreed with me that there was no time to waste because of a possible civil suit against Ryan. The tape was found in the girl's bedroom closet and is now at police headquarters. Just to be on the safe side, I convinced the chief to allow me to make a copy of it. Now there's no way that those parents will be able to bleed Ryan for money because of what his son did. Don't get me wrong, Debra, I feel sorry for them, but at least now Ryan won't be forced to suffer financially as well as emotionally thanks to you. Regardless of what you may think of him, he is a good person."

"So good, in fact," Debra said, "that he told me he was going to have you drop the lawsuit against me."

"Doesn't surprise me in the least." Bert raised his cup of coffee and looked at her over the rim. "I know you're probably not going to answer this question, but I'm going to ask it anyway. How is all of this going to affect your crusade against Ryan in particular and the weapons industry in general?" He drank some coffee, placed the cup on the table, and leaned forward to hear what she might say.

"It goes without saying that these murders definitely underscore the need for my crusade against violence to be stepped up. And we both know that the firearms industry is far from blameless in the matter. But as far as singling out Ryan for any future detrimental columns, no, that's not going to happen. Even if you and he hadn't told me you were backing away from the lawsuit, he deserves the chance to try to get his life back together as best he can without me sniping at him."

Bert smiled. "He'll be relieved to hear that. I know for a fact that he's been worried about having to lay off some of his employees if his business suffered because of your columns. That's the only reason he wanted me to file suit in the first place. You can give him the good news when we go back up there."

"I'll have to ask you to tell him yourself," Debra said. "I still have a lot more people I'd like to talk to while all of their emotions are still fresh."

"What you're telling me is that Debra Dunn's News Views doesn't write itself."

"Something like that. Although the opinions in my column are mine, they are certainly influenced by those of everyone I speak with. I think of my column not as a soapbox, but rather as a means of getting my readers to think about and talk about issues."

"Now that we're no longer playing on opposing teams, I don't mind admitting that I try never to miss reading one of your columns."

She smiled. "And I bet now that you know your client will not suffer any more of my diatribes, you'll be even more supportive of my work."

"Guilty as charged," he said.

She smiled. "It's gratifying to hear that at least one person in Thomasville won't be canceling any newspaper subscriptions because of my stand against your town's biggest employer." She finished her drink and pushed her chair slightly away from the table. "I really do need to get back to work." Debra extended her hand across the table. "Bert, it was nice to meet you, and I hope you won't hold it against me for ruining your chances to go to war against Geoff Billings and all the newspaper publishers."

He shook her hand. "Can't say that I hadn't been looking forward to it, but that would have been business, and what you did today for Ryan was personal. I don't know if you're aware that I have a reputation for being a hard-ass in legal circles, but I will never forget that you may well have saved Ryan's company today." He took out his wallet, and for a fleeting moment, Debra thought he was going to insult her by handing her some money for delivering the letter from Luke. But all the attorney did was pass one of his business cards across the table. "Debra, if you ever have a problem that I can help you with—and I don't mean just a legal matter—call me and I'll do everything in my power to help you out. And despite the reputation we lawyers have for being financial parasites, my services won't cost you a penny." He grinned. "But don't worry about me going hungry; I'll just chase the next ambulance a little faster."

DEBRA DUNN'S NEWS VIEWS

One of the first columns I wrote denouncing Ryan Cordell dealt with a funeral for a baby and her young mother who had been killed with a weapon made by the Cordell Firearms Company. That funeral had been held in Chicago. The funeral I attended today took place in Thomasville, Illinois. This time the funeral service was held for three family members instead of two.

The good-byes and prayers for Elaine, Caitlin, and Luke Cordell were every bit as sad as the ones for the mother and baby in Chicago, and rightly so. The heartbreaking series of events that led to this tragedy have dominated the news since the story broke. There is no useful purpose to be served by rehashing those events here. The focus of this column is the lone survivor of the Cordell family.

Despite the business that Ryan Cordell owns and operates, the loss of his entire family and his paralysis should not be viewed as justified. Ironic, to be sure, but no person deserves to endure a tragedy of that magnitude.

There is another irony, an irony that involves me, and one which I would never have mentioned had it not been headlined in countless newspapers and reported on just about every single radio and TV news program. Most of those people reporting the news that I had turned over to Ryan Cordell's attorney a letter written by Luke Cordell, tied that letter in with the dismissal of a lawsuit that had been filed against me. Any reader who chooses to believe that my motive was self-serving is entitled to do so. I would prefer losing every single one of my readers to not having had the opportunity to see the look in Ryan Cordell's eyes when he read that explanatory letter from his son.

Although my campaign against violence in this country will continue, it will no longer single out any one individual, any one company, any one organization. There is enough blame out there to be spread evenly and universally.

Insofar as Ryan Cordell is concerned, I would ask all of you at this time to think of him as a man, not as a businessman. I don't care whether you are a member of the gun lobby, or if you feel exactly as I do about the matter, I ask each of you to mail a personal message to Ryan Cordell expressing your hopes and prayers for him to successfully deal with this tragedy.

CHAPTER TEN

The days following the loss of his family had Ryan Cordell fluctuating between complete sorrow and utter despair. It was a testament to his character that only a minute portion of those emotions involved his paralysis. In the succeeding weeks he threw his energies into his physical therapy to a degree that had his therapists cautioning him to take it slower. But he was determined to become as self-sufficient as possible as quickly as he could manage.

What Ryan could not manage was to continue living in the house where the tragedy had taken place. He had also decided that his company would no longer manufacture firearms. Neither would he allow the organization he'd founded continue to exist. GUN was disbanded, and Ryan converted that building into his living quarters. Since it was situated right alongside his factory, it was an ideal location for him. Although he temporarily laid off many of his employees, he promised to rehire them as soon as he could retool the factory to produce products other than weapons. This process was a time-consuming one for a multitude of reasons. And now, a little over eight months since his life had been irrevocably changed, more than three-fourths of his employees were back to work, but he wouldn't rest until that figure reached one hundred percent.

The sun felt comfortable on Ryan's bare arms as he slowly rolled his wheelchair across the factory parking lot toward the new van that had been delivered that morning. The driver from the dealership that specialized in converting vans for handicapped drivers had driven away in the hand-operated van that Ryan had bought used during the course of his physical therapy. But he wasn't trading in that vehicle. He had asked the owner of the dealership to hand over the used van free of charge to the customer who could least afford to pay for a specialized van.

Ryan maneuvered his wheelchair around the perimeter of the new van as he inspected it for the second time that day. He stopped near the sliding door, opened it, and then lowered the electric lift.

"Look who has a new toy," Bert Dupont said as he walked to Ryan's side as the metal platform touched the pavement.

"Yeah, I'm the envy of all the other kids in my neighborhood," Ryan said dryly.

The attorney looked around at the factory, the converted former headquarters of GUN, and the wooded area across the road. "Seems to me like you're the *only* kid living in this neighborhood."

"Uh huh, and that's just the way I like it."

Bert frowned without realizing he was doing it. "You really have to start getting out around other people more often. Ryan, why don't you go to dinner with Betty and me tonight?"

Ryan chuckled. "I think your wife has seen a lot more of me than she cares to over these last few months. Let's not subject her to another threesome for dinner again tonight."

"She enjoys your company and you know it, you big faker." He gave Ryan a sly look, which he didn't catch because he was staring up into the interior of his new van. "And, anyway, it wouldn't have to be a threesome. Betty has mentioned that more than one available lady she knows has asked her if she thought you might consider becoming socially active again."

"Damn it! Bert, look at how I have to get around. I'm *never* going to be socially active again as you so euphemistically phrase it. And I'm surprised at Betty. She's much too intelligent not to realize that any woman asking her about me is interested only in my bank account. I have nothing else to offer a woman since it happened. If Betty sent you over here today to play matchmaker, tell her for me that it was a fool's errand."

"For your information, I'm the one who thinks it's time for you to start going out with women; Betty thinks you're far from ready to even consider it."

"Well, she's right."

"But not for the reason you mentioned. She knows how much you loved Elaine—still love Elaine—and that you no doubt feel you'll never be capable of loving someone else. You're wrong, of course, and one of these days you'll figure that out."

"Don't count on it," Ryan said.

"And don't you count on being right about women being interested in you for your money. Don't try to tell me that Elaine married you for your money."

"No, but I was still a man back then." Ryan blinked, and then blinked again before averting his eyes.

"Cut the crap! You know as well as I do that any man can please a woman without using his freakin' pecker . . . and often a hell of a lot more. Just keep that in mind when you finally are ready to go out with women again." The excitable lawyer began to hyperventilate and took a few steps away from Ryan as if to calm himself down. Then he abruptly returned. "Man, I think I'd be willing to put my dick out to pasture if I could be just half as handsome as you are."

"Aw, Bert, we both know you don't mean that," Ryan said. He grinned then and reached up to thump Bert's shoulder with his fist. "But I do appreciate you trying in your own charming way to make me feel better about a chapter of my life that's closed."

"Humph. The reason I'm here happens to concern a chapter of your life that you may have thought was closed. But I'm going to reopen it."

Ryan's expression darkened. "Bert, if this is about those firearms companies trying to get me to sign an agreement to let them use the Cordell name and my patents, the answer is still 'no.' That part of my life is over forever."

"Come on, Ryan. Give me a little more credit than that. I came here to talk to you about Debra Dunn."

"Debra?" Ryan looked puzzled for a moment. "Oh, I get it. Her wedding's now about two weeks away and she called you to convince you to bug me about changing my mind. She called me the same day she got my reply stating I wasn't going to attend. There's nothing you can say that's going to convince me to go. Sitting in this chair in some banquet hall while everyone else is dancing is not my ideal way to spend an evening." Ryan looked into the open door of his new van, and it didn't take a mind reader to know he wanted to end this conversation and get back to checking out the vehicle.

"No, Ryan, I haven't heard anything from Debra. I thought it was awfully nice of her to invite Betty and me to her wedding. And I had been looking forward to it until I got a call from an associate of mine late last night."

"Some lawyer called you and advised you not to go to Debra Dunn's wedding? Is he representing a firearms manufacturer that is being harassed in her column? Does he want to give your firm a piece of the action?"

"Damn it! Even if you've forgotten how Debra saved your ass back then, I haven't. The guy who called me last night wasn't an attorney."

"I'm sorry, Bert. I shouldn't have said that. Who called you last night?"

"I'm not going to give you his name. But I will tell you that he was one of the private investigators I used back when we were trying to dig up dirt on Debra for the lawsuit."

"Hold it right there. Even though I'm not going to her wedding, I can honestly say that I admire and respect the woman, Bert. If whatever dirt your PI dug up about her makes you want to change your plans about going, that's your business. But do me a favor and keep that information to yourself. I don't want to hear it."

Bert Dupont removed an audio cassette from his pocket and held it in front of Ryan. "I paid the guy a sizable fee for driving here from Parkerton this morning to deliver this. After you listen to it I'm sure you'll agree it was worth every penny."

With her wedding only a few weeks away, Debra was getting more nervous with each passing day. All of the responses were now in her possession, and the only refusal had come from Ryan Cordell. Although she hadn't regretted phoning him to attempt to cajole him into coming, she had been very disappointed. She had felt that the brief time they'd spent together on the day she delivered the letter from his son heralded the start of a unique sort of friendship. But since any friendship requires two willing participants, that was not to be.

Sitting there in front of her computer as she tried to focus on writing her column, Debra let her mind shift from the one person who had chosen not to attend her wedding to the many people who would be there. First and foremost, she needed her father to lean on and share her happiness as she embarked on that new phase of her life. Bill Overfield had beaten his daughter to the altar by more than five months and was thriving in his new life with Abby. As Abby had wanted, their wedding had been held in the newly refurbished Victorian house with only a handful of people in attendance. Although her inherited wealth would have permitted them to honeymoon anywhere in the world and for any length of time, they chose a one-week cruise in the Caribbean. Upon their return, Debra could tell that her father and her brand-new stepmother had become even closer—something she hadn't thought possible.

Debra sighed as she stared at the blinking cursor on the mostly-empty monitor screen. Knowing she definitely wasn't in the mood to finish writing the column, she saved the text and then left the office next to her bedroom and went downstairs to sit on the sofa in the living room. Her mind immediately went back to her former musings. Without a doubt, her father and Abby were perfectly suited to be together. The depth of their love was apparent to anyone with the slightest degree of sensitivity. There was one thing that Debra had sensed about Abby, however, that had unsettled the bride-to-be when she discussed it with her stepmother.

On numerous occasions, Debra had felt that Abby had reservations about Carl Manning—reservations that she did not want to share with Debra or anyone else. Finally, just one week ago, Debra had asked Abby to meet her for lunch on a day when Bill had other plans. It took a maximum of persuasion on Debra's part, but Abby finally admitted that Carl reminded her of some of the shallow, phony people—both male and female— that she had encountered while socializing with her first husband in Beverly Hills and Hollywood. She had gone on to assure Debra that these misgivings probably could be attributable to Carl's striking good looks and laid-back mannerisms. Debra had tried valiantly not to be hurt by Abby's assessment of her future husband, but had been only partially successful. She was positive that Abby would realize she had been mistaken after she and Carl had been married for awhile. It was a credit to both women that that luncheon discussion did nothing to impair their relationship.

Debra looked at the late-morning sunshine streaming into the living room and briefly entertained the idea of going for a long walk. Instead of acting on the impulse, she remained seated on the sofa and pictured her wedding day. Jim Hopkins and his wife would be coming up from Florida to attend. She was looking forward to talking over old times with her former boss. There would always be a special place in her heart for the man who had taught her so much about the newspaper business.

Geoff Billings, her present employer, would also be in attendance. He—Debra was certain—would make his appearance with a trophy date on his arm, but she didn't hold that against him. That was his chosen lifestyle, and he lived it to the hilt. She smiled as she pictured herself teasing him about how young his date was sure to be. Debra liked Geoff as much as Jim, but in different ways and for different reasons. The phone rang, and she was still wearing the smile as she answered it.

"Hello, Debra. This is Ryan."

"Ryan?"

"Ryan Cordell. The bum who turned down your wedding invitation."

She laughed. "Ryan, I hope you're not feeling guilty over that. As I told you when we spoke, I would have loved it if you came, but I understand how you feel. I honestly do." There was such a long silence that she asked, "Ryan, you still there?"

"Yes, I'm still here." Another pause, but shorter. "Debra, would it be possible for me to talk you into having lunch with me?"

This time it was Debra who hesitated. "Uh . . . well, sure. I don't see why not. Of course, I am pretty busy, what with the wedding so close, but anytime after we get back from our honeymoon would be fine. I'm sure Carl would like to meet you."

"Debra, I have to see you right away."

"Ryan, you don't sound right. What's wrong? Your . . . your condition hasn't gotten worse I hope."

"No, my condition is the same as it has been. Debra, this is really important. I need to see you today."

"Lunch today?" She looked at her watch. "Ryan, it's almost noon now, and by the time I drive to Thomasville it will be—"

"You don't have to drive anywhere. Look out your window."

Debra stood and looked at the street and saw the unfamiliar van parked in front of her house. "Are you in that van?"

"I am."

"Who drove you here? Bert?"

Ryan chuckled. "No. I drove myself. They make all sorts of handy gadgets for people who can't use their legs."

"That was incredibly stupid of me. I'm sorry, Ryan."

"Don't be. I should have phoned you first from home, but I didn't want to give you the time to think about refusing. Will you please come out now?"

"I'll be right there."

Debra hung up the phone and went outside. She smiled as she opened the door and climbed into the van. "This is quite a surprise," she said as she buckled herself in and he started the engine.

"For me as well," he said as he drove away from the curb.

She glanced at the hand-operated controls and the restraints holding the wheelchair before returning her eyes to the road. "It's all right to be curious," he assured her. "People don't see this sort of setup every day of the week. Please don't be nervous. I've had a lot of practice driving this way. I started a few weeks after it happened."

"Really? This van looks and smells like it just came out of the showroom."

"You're absolutely right. This one did. It was delivered to me yesterday. I had a used one before this."

"I see." Since she'd been told it wouldn't be offensive, she studied the controls closely. "I'm guessing it was difficult to learn how to drive."

"Not really. No doubt it would be harder for you than it had been for me." She looked at him and raised her eyebrows. He smiled. "No, I don't mean because I'm a better driver or that you're not a guy. It's just that when you can't move your legs, you're not reflexively trying to slam on the breaks with your foot." He looked briefly at her face before returning his attention to the road.

Debra saw the concern in his expression. "Ryan, why are you here?"

"I told you. I wanted to take you out to lunch." He smiled. She saw it was forced.

"No. Really, Ryan. There's something you want to tell me. What is it?"

He didn't respond, at least not verbally. She felt the speed increasing and knew he was exceeding the limit. Looking at the speedometer, she saw that they were going forty-five in a twenty-five zone. "Ryan, slow down before you get a ticket." Again he said nothing. And again he started going even faster. "Ryan, you're starting to make me nervous. Please slow down."

She looked ahead at a diner they were rapidly approaching. "Stop at that restaurant and we can have our lunch there."

"No. I'm going to get on the Interstate."

She knew that the entrance to the highway was less than half a mile past the diner. Debra also knew there were no restaurants on the Interstate for the first seventy miles. The emotion that was overtaking her was an unfamiliar one—fear. "Ryan, I've changed my mind. Please take me home."

Debra felt the van slow down and was relieved. He was going to turn around and drive her home. But then she realized he had slowed only to make the sharp turn onto the highway. She briefly considered jumping out of the van as it went into the turn, but knew she would end up injured or worse. The van entered the Interstate and was soon going at the speed limit of sixty-five. She saw him press a button, which she correctly assumed to be the cruise control. He visibly relaxed as they sped along the highway.

"Ryan, why are you doing this to me? I thought you were my friend."

"I *am* your friend, Debra. And that's why it was necessary for me so talk to you today."

"Talking is one thing, Ryan, but what you're doing comes dangerously close to kidnapping." She saw his jaw clench after she made the statement.

"I'm truly sorry about that, but I was afraid you wouldn't listen to everything I came to tell you if I didn't do something dramatic like this."

"What could you possibly have to tell me that makes it necessary to be speeding down a highway when you say it?"

"You have to call off your wedding. Debra, you can't marry Carl Manning."

"Call off my wedding?" she said in a tone appropriately suited to the absurdity. "Have you lost your mind?" He turned toward her just long enough for her to see his sad expression. She was certain that sadness had nothing to do with her assessment of his mental condition, and everything to do with his

193

romantic feelings for her. She was instantly contrite. "Oh, Ryan." Debra sighed and then took a deep breath, more to stall for time than to speak the words she knew must be said. "Ryan, I'm flattered; truly I am. I suspected that you might have feelings for me when I read your negative response to my wedding invitation. When I first began my crusade against your company and your organization, I never dreamed that I would so quickly come to think of you as a friend. But I love Carl. Surely you understand that I—"

"Carl Manning doesn't love you," Ryan spat. "He only wants to marry you so that he can use your money to buy the health club where he works. He plans to divorce you as soon as it's a done deal."

"That's completely absurd." Debra looked at the determined set of Ryan's jaw as he removed an audio cassette from his shirt pocket.

"You're going to change your mind after you hear the man himself admitting it," he said.

As Ryan reached over to insert the cassette in the player, Debra tried to snatch it out of his hand. "Now I *know* you're crazy!"

He deftly withdrew the tape from her reach. "I may be stuck in this wheelchair for the rest of my life, but the top half of my body works just as well as ever."

Frustrated, Debra settled once again against the back of her seat. "Look at you," she said. "You're actually sitting there grinning. What did you do, hire some guy to impersonate Carl's voice to get me to call off my wedding so that you could make a play for me?"

"I'm sorry if I was smiling. I guess it was just an unconscious reaction to being with someone I like—someone I never thought I would see again. But, Debra, we both know I'm useless in the romance department, so please don't ever accuse me of coming to you with this heartbreaking news because I haven't come to terms with the fact that the romantic portion of my life is over. And, no, the tape, I'm sorry to say, is not a fake."

Debra was about to respond to that mindset in virtually the same manner that Bert Dupont had on the previous day. Instead, she looked at his expression that no longer had any evidence of a grin, and said nothing. After they drove along in silence for a few seconds, she asked, "For the sake of argument, let's say that I believe you have a tape of Carl saying those horrible things about his reason for marrying me. Are you expecting me to believe that he would call you, of all people, and disclose something like that?"

"No, of course not. I got the tape yesterday from Bert."

"Your attorney Bert?"

"Yes. My attorney, and my friend. And more importantly, your friend."

Debra mulled this over for a few seconds. "So now I'm expected to believe that Carl phoned your attorney to disclose his devious intentions? Ryan, I have to tell you, none of this is making any sense whatsoever."

"I know, Debra. I know. I suppose it would have been a lot smarter of me if I'd asked Bert to break this rotten news to you. I'm positive he'd have done a much better job of it than I am. But I just felt I owe you so much for having given me the letter from Luke that I wanted to be the one to personally save you from making such a huge mistake."

When Ryan glanced at her, Debra took that opportunity to search his face for even the slightest hint of guile, and couldn't find any. There was now a feeling of doubt starting to creep into Debra's thoughts, and she was ashamed to admit to herself that that doubt concerned Carl instead of Ryan. "How exactly did Bert come into possession of that tape?" Debra pointed at the cassette that Ryan still held in his right hand as she asked the question.

"Bert was informed of the tape by the man who recorded it. He is a private detective who had been hired to gather information about an entirely different matter."

"I see. Can you tell me what the different matter is, or has Bert sworn you to secrecy for legal reasons concerning some lawsuit he's working on?"

"Bert's not involved in it. The PI had been hired to sniff out some information about illegal steroid use by bodybuilders and the people who supplied them."

"Now I'm to believe that Carl is a criminal as well as a man who was only going to marry me so I could be tricked into buying the health club for him?"

"No, Carl was clean so far as the steroids were concerned. In fact, the PI suspected Carl's friend and coworker, Peter Hatch, more than he did Carl. Hatch, as it turned out, also is doing nothing illegal. But it was during a conversation with Peter Hatch and Carl Manning at a bar in Parkerton that the detective recorded this tape." Ryan moved the tape to a position halfway between the steering wheel and the player. He looked inquisitively at Debra.

"Play the tape," she said.

As soon as the sound started emerging from the speakers, Debra felt apprehensive. The first voice she heard belonged to a man who was not known to her, so that had to be the detective. The next man to speak made a derogatory remark about a woman who had apparently walked by. "That was Pete," she said, more to herself than to Ryan. Although it was fairly faint, she could tell that the background noise seemed to be that heard in a typical bar. When Carl spoke there wasn't the slightest doubt in her mind whose voice it was. That was bad enough, but when she heard his derisive tone as he began confirming everything Ryan had warned her about, she was devastated.

Ryan took his eyes off the road long enough to confirm his suspicion that Debra was crying. He saw that she was staring at the tape player, not in disbelief, but with disappointment. She looked over at him then. The compassion in his expression made her unable to suppress a ragged sob, but her resolve kept any more of them to make their way out of her chest.

"I'm sorry, Debra. I'll turn it off."

"No!" she shouted. His hand retreated to the steering wheel.

It wasn't too many more seconds after that that the speakers became silent. In a very gentle tone, Ryan said, "That's the end of it, Debra. It's over."

"Yes," she said. "It's over."

Ryan Cordell leaned slightly forward and to his right and ejected the tape.

Kerry Deminski

CHAPTER ELEVEN

More than half the tables were empty in the restaurant side of the establishment, but Debra could see through the connecting doorway that the bar was crowded. Since the bar was one of Parkerton's favorite weekend hangouts for single people, there was no reason why this Saturday night should be any different from any other. Debra thought of the many nights she had spent in there with Carl Manning while they were dating, but she was a married woman now and those days were nothing but a bittersweet memory.

Debra felt a substantial movement inside her womb and she jerked slightly in her chair as her hand moved from the table to her abdomen.

"Looks like one of the twins just gave you a nasty kick," Abby said from across the table.

Abby's husband, Bill, smiled at his daughter as Debra's other hand moved to the opposite side of her expansive midsection. "I'm guessing both of them are kicking up a storm tonight. They must be as hungry for this seafood dinner as you are," he said.

Debra returned her father's smile. "They're not kicking, but they are restless tonight. Maybe they know they'll be seeing what this world looks like in six more weeks and can't contain their curiosity."

"I'm just as curious as they are," Debra's husband said as he reached over to give her abdomen an affectionate pat. "I can't wait to see how they look and how they act and what kind of people they're going to become."

Debra laughed. "Slow down, Ryan. We have a lot of diaper changing and sleepless nights to get through before it's time for college, careers and wedding bells."

"She's right, Ryan," Bill Overfield said as he placed his wineglass back on the table. "I'm sure you haven't forgotten those nights back when your own kids were—"

Bill, realizing his blunder, broke off his sentence a heartbeat before his wife sharply drew in a breath. Debra saw the anguish in her father's expression as he said, "Oh God. Ryan, that was incredibly stupid of me. I'm sorry. And I've only had one sip of wine so I can't use alcohol as an excuse for my insensitivity."

"You were just making conversation, Bill. Don't go beating yourself up over it," Ryan said. "All of us have lost people we've loved dearly, and it's only natural for those loved ones to come up in conversation every once in a while." He raised his glass and held it out toward his father-in-law. "Let's drink a toast to the people we love, whether they live with us in this world or now live only in our hearts." Bill and the two women lightly clinked glasses with Ryan as they murmured some appropriate words. While all of the glasses were on their way back to the table, Ryan said, "I'm beginning to wonder if the chef is back in the kitchen toasting his waiters instead of preparing our meals. I'm starving."

"I've held a few waitress jobs way back when," Abby said, "and I'd never encountered a chef who gave the servers anything except a hard time."

"Sounds like a few of the supervisors I've had at the post office," Bill chimed in.

"Don't you go looking for any sympathy from me," Abby teased. "Back in my nursing days, I guarantee that most of the doctors I encountered gave me more grief than any postal supervisor ever dished out to you."

"Oh, sure," Bill countered. "That's why there have been so many incidents of disgruntled nurses shooting up the hospitals they work in." Because this reference to violence was more generalized than the reminder of the loss of Ryan's children, Bill Overfield hadn't even thought about it upsetting anyone at the table.

"Ah, here comes our food," Debra said as their waiter approached their table balancing a huge circular tray on one hand.

The meal progressed in a leisurely manner and was nearing the point when thoughts of dessert began popping up in their minds. "I'm trying to decide whether to order the chocolate mousse or their apple dumpling with vanilla ice cream," Debra said. Even though she had never been pregnant, Abby smiled knowingly. Bill also smiled at his daughter; he was very pleased that he was finally going to become a grandfather.

"No need to decide," Ryan told his wife. "I'll order one and you order the other. You can have as much of mine as you want."

Debra was about to make a comment about how much weight she had put on during her pregnancy when she heard a familiar voice from behind her chair. "Well, well, well. Isn't he just the sweetest thing? First he talks you out of marrying me, and now he offers to share his dessert. What a prize catch."

Debra's eyes were wide with surprise as she looked up into Carl Manning's face. That face looked slightly doughy as if he had both increased his caloric intake and decreased his exercise regimen since she'd last seen him. She couldn't help but wonder if that noticeable change could be a result of his disappointment over losing her as his meal ticket. The health club had been sold—to someone else—and friends had informed her that Carl still worked as manager of the facility. There was little doubt in her mind that her former lover resented her for dumping him and ruining his opportunity to use her funds to purchase the club. But the way the man was glaring at her husband showed that Ryan was resented at least as much—if not more—as she.

"Carl, please go back to your table or the bar or wherever you were," Debra said. "We're here to enjoy a pleasant evening. Don't spoil it."

Carl turned away from Ryan and smiled at Debra. "When have you ever known me to spoil anything? Isn't that your specialty, Deb?" Without giving her time to respond, he looked at the couple seated across the table. "You're looking really happy, Bill. Is that because you ended up marrying a rich widow or because Debra is gonna make you a grandpa? Too bad you will never know who the father of her baby is. I hear those sperm banks don't give out that information."

Bill Overfield was in the process of jumping to his feet with the intention of charging around the table to physically confront the obnoxious intruder. Although Abby put a restraining hand on his arm, it was Ryan who convinced him to reluctantly sit back on his chair. "Don't do it, Bill. This jerk would like nothing better than having you take a poke or two at him so he could sue and still try to make some money from your family. Believe me, guys like him aren't worth slugging no matter how much they deserve it."

Carl leaned down, snatched up Debra's glass of wine, and tossed the liquid into Ryan's face. Ryan's blink reflex prevented most of the wine from entering his eyes, but enough had seeped through his eyelids to cause some stinging.

"I'm going to call the police," Debra announced as she stood and began to move between her chair and Carl.

"You're not going to call anybody. Sit down and shut up," Carl snarled. He gave her a shove to implement his command. Debra was knocked off balance, due as much to her ungainly size as to his rough treatment.

"No!" Abby screamed as Debra's left temple solidly hit the edge of the table. The pregnant woman's body struck the chair, toppling it over as she fell to the floor.

Neither his wife nor Ryan could have possibly then prevented Bill from becoming involved at that point. He pushed away from the table and scrambled around it. Ryan did not wait for his father-in-law to arrive. He reached up and grabbed Carl's tie with his left hand. After yanking the startled man's head down into range, Ryan delivered a powerful right to the jaw. Abby saw Carl's head snap back and pull his tie free of Ryan's grip. She wasn't sure if the sound she heard that sounded like a breaking bone issued from Carl's jaw or Ryan's hand. But there was no doubt in her mind that the unwanted visitor was unconscious before he crumpled to the floor. As she rushed around the table to assist Debra, Abby had the fleeting thought that the months of using his arms to push his weight around in his wheelchair had served Ryan well during this unexpected encounter.

Ryan sat helplessly as he watched Abby kneel alongside Debra. The former nurse had already dispatched Bill to call for an ambulance. Ryan knew that the police would also become involved and he had little doubt that Carl Manning would attempt to use the legal system to gain monetary compensation for his injury. But that was a matter for Bert Dupont to handle. Uppermost in Ryan's mind was his fear for his wife's health and that of his unborn twins. He didn't want to even consider the possibility of losing his second family. But the thoughts of his former career as the owner of a firearms factory didn't allow him the luxury of dismissing that frightening possibility.

EPILOGUE

DEBRA DUNN'S NEWS VIEWS

The news in this particular column is of a more personal nature than anything I've ever written before. So personal, in fact, that I felt it necessary to seek my husband's approval before making some of the disclosures. Those of you who read this column on a regular basis know that my husband, Ryan Cordell, suffered the loss of his children and first wife during a tragedy that also resulted in the loss of his ability to walk. Although I love Ryan with an intensity that words simply cannot express, I would forgo that love in a heartbeat if doing so could change his past. But since no one can change the past, I'll do my very best to see that his future is filled with love and happiness.

I am sitting up in my hospital bed as I'm writing this. The sounds filtering into my room through the closed door are subdued now as midnight is only moments away. Ryan managed to stay long after visiting hours ended, but I finally shooed him out to go home and get some much-needed rest. I'm exhausted too, but too excited to sleep. My twins were born at eight thirty-six and eight thirty-nine this morning, and I have yet to come down from my cloud of euphoria. Alicia and Ethan are sleeping in the nursery just a few doors away from my room, but I miss them as much as if they were in a distant country.

Ryan and I will be forever grateful to the doctors at the fertility clinic for performing the procedures making it possible for Ryan to become the father of a second family. How happy I would be for my husband and all the other people in the world with spinal cord injuries if science can someday reverse the paralysis they endure. The breakthroughs that medical science makes so regularly makes that possibility seem not too farfetched.

The clock has just ticked to one minute after midnight, so it is officially the second day of life in the outside world for my babies.   And I'm officially crying.   But in case anybody is concerned, the tears are the result of postpartum happiness, not postpartum depression.

This will be the last column I'll be writing for awhile so that I can spend some time getting to know Ethan and Alicia. My boss, Geoffrey Billings, has graciously told me to take off as many weeks as I need. And I promised him that I would. But he knows—and I hope all of you know—that sharing my views with you of the world we live in will call me back to work soon. Until that time, I'd like to sincerely thank all of you for your loyalty shown by continuing to read my columns. One of the walls of my room here is almost completely covered with printouts of congratulatory e-mails you have sent me. Your sentiments are deeply appreciated. What will be appreciated by all of my editors is for me to wrap up this already overly long column.

Now I'm finally ready to sleep.

ABOUT THE AUTHOR

It is a well-documented fact that a fiction writer's life experiences enhance the plots and characters that he or she creates. Kerry Deminski is a man who worked as a letter carrier for the United States Postal Service for three and a half decades, but also spent a lot of time before and during that period holding down other jobs as well. He worked as an armed guard for a detective agency, as a truck driver for a bookbinder, as a janitor, as a heating and air conditioning mechanic, as a theater usher, as a convenience store clerk, as a factory laborer. While still a teenager in Appalachia, he spent three years working after high school and on weekends for an uncle in the trucking business, shoveling coal and delivering ice into hundreds of homes in that financially-depressed region.

During these jobs, and others not mentioned, Deminski filed away in his mind all of the people he met and the things they said and did, hoping to draw upon these experiences to enrich the books he knew he would write someday. Now that someday has arrived, and the prolific author turns out one, sometimes two, novels every year.

Kerry Deminski has also received royalties for song lyrics he has written; he has sold humor to *Playboy Magazine*; he has been granted U.S. Patent Numbers 5,755,438 and 5,788,706 for two of his inventions.

Books written by Kerry Deminski

1. ATONEMENT
2. CANCELED WITH BLOOD:
   A POST OFFICE MASSACRE
3. FAVORITE SON
4. A GHOST FOR SYLVIA
5. IN HARD COAL COUNTRY
6. MINOR OBSESSION

www.ingramcontent.com/pod-product-compliance
Lightning Source LLC
Chambersburg PA
CBHW030314290526
45785CB00001B/360